Minnesota's
Twentieth Century

D. J. Tice

Minnesota's
Twentieth Century

STORIES OF

EXTRAORDINARY

EVERYDAY

PEOPLE

University of Minnesota Press   Minneapolis / London

Published in cooperation with the *St. Paul Pioneer Press*

Photographs from the Iron Range Research Center in the chapter "Save Your Breath and Start Climbing: The Milford Mine Disaster, 1924" are from the Croft Mine Park Collection, the Vienna Maki Collection, and the Anthony Addy Collection, all at the Iron Range Research Center, Chisholm, Minnesota.

Photographs from Howard Sivertson in the chapter "Lost Island: Isle Royale Fishing" are from his book *Once upon an Isle,* published by the Wisconsin Folk Museum, copyright 1992.

Library of Congress Cataloging-in-Publication Data
Tice, D. J.
    Minnesota's twentieth century : stories of extraordinary everyday people / D. J. Tice.
        p.   cm.
    "Published in cooperation with the *St. Paul Pioneer Press*."
    "Essays in this book were originally published as 'A century of stories,' a feature series in the *St. Paul Pioneer Press* from 1997 to 1999"—T. p. verso.
    ISBN 0-8166-3428-9 (acid-free paper). —ISBN 0-8166-3429-7 (pbk. : acid-free paper)
    1. Minnesota—History—20th century Anecdotes. 2. Minnesota Biography Anecdotes. I. Title.
F606.6.T53   1999
977.6'05—dc21   99–29883

Published by the University of Minnesota Press
111 Third Avenue South, Suite 290
Minneapolis, MN 55401-2520
http://www.upress.umn.edu

Printed in the United States of America on acid-free paper
Designed by Diane Gleba Hall
The University of Minnesota is an equal-opportunity educator and employer.

11 10 09 08 07 06 05 04 03 02 01 00 99   10 9 8 7 6 5 4 3 2 1

For Cindy, the happy ending of my own story.

Contents

ix **ACKNOWLEDGMENTS**

xi **PROLOGUE**
The Special Feeling We Had

3 **INTRODUCTION: RAPIDS IN THE STREAM OF TIME**
The Dawn of the Twentieth Century, 1901

10 **THE LAST HANGING**
The Gottschalk and Williams Murder Cases, 1905

18 **UNSAFE FOR DEMOCRACY**
The World War I Loyalty Crusade, 1917

28 **PEACE AND DEATH**
The Influenza Pandemic, 1918

36 **A LOT OF PREACHERS, A LOT OF GANGSTERS**
Prohibition, 1920

44 **THE MOST ATROCIOUS CRIME**
The Duluth Lynchings, 1920

54 **SAVE YOUR BREATH AND START CLIMBING**
The Milford Mine Disaster, 1924

62 **ANOTHER COUNTRY**
Life on and off the Reservation

72 **DUST BOWL SISTERS**
The Great Depression, 1934

82 **GREAT GOVERNORS**
Johnson, Olson, and Stassen

94 **A HAVE-NOT'S WAR**
The Spanish Civil War, 1937–38

102 **LOST ISLAND**
Isle Royale Fishing

112 **BARBED-WIRE WARRIORS**
The POWs' Secret War, 1943–45

122 **IRON LADY**
The Voice of the Range

132 **ARE YOU COLORED?**
Discrimination and Progress

140 **WHERE THE ACTION WAS**
Wars Hot and Cold

148 **A CERTAIN DISTANCE**
"The Sixties"

156 **SOLDIER'S HEART**
Vietnam, 1968

166 **WHO THE HELL IS KEN DAHLBERG?**
Watergate, 1972

176 **ON EAGLE'S WINGS**
The Long Journey of a Hockey Legend

186 **HAUNTED EXILES**
Saigon to Minneapolis

196 **ROOT CAUSES**
The Farm Crisis That Never Ended

ACKNOWLEDGMENTS

A collection of memories is by its nature a collaboration. The writer of such a work is a recorder more than a creator. I can never repay my debt to the Minnesotans who shared their experiences and knowledge with me for *Minnesota's Twentieth Century*. They are the real authors of this book.

I wish to thank my editors on this project at the *St. Paul Pioneer Press,* particularly Walker Lundy and Sue Campbell. Their support for an oddball history project by an opinion page writer they hardly knew at the outset reflects the daredevil passion for ideas that keeps our newspaper original and audacious.

I'm grateful as well for the creative contributions of editors Kathy Derong, Bob McIntosh, and Cheryl Burch-Schoff, designers Larry May, Ellen Simonson, and Marcia Roepke, reporter Richard Chin, and the many *Pioneer Press* photographers whose sensitive work appears throughout this book. The *Pioneer Press* library staff has, as always, been tireless and resourceful. My colleagues on the opinion pages, especially editor Ron Clark, have been steadfastly supportive, graciously enduring my distractions.

The staff of the Minnesota Historical Society provided sound advice, able research assistance, and critical help finding subjects. Special thanks to Barbara Averill, Jim Fogerty, Patrick Coleman, Mark Greene, and Bonnie Wilson. I'm also indebted for indispensable research help to Ed Nelson and other staff at the Iron Range Research Center in Chisholm, Minnesota.

Many generous people, in addition to those mentioned above and below, helped me find the subjects of this book. Without that aid the project would have been impossible. Thanks to Stephen B. Young (whose expert interpreting was also an invaluable kindness), Beth Christensen and her class at Mankato's Dakota Meadows Middle School, Kent Nerburn, Carl Chrislock, Pam Leschak, Michael Fedo, Marlin Bree, Mike Sweeney, Mark Mulvihill, William Hull, Sue Phillips, Don Boxmeyer, and Bonnie Blodgett.

The book also owes its existence to the perseverance of Todd Orjala, my editor at the University of Minnesota Press. His skill and commitment to excellence have been a constant comfort.

I'm uniquely indebted to two longtime friends and colleagues, Dan Kelly and Greg Breining, who expressed enthusiasm and offered insightful advice from this project's early, tentative stages. I well recall sheltering from a frigid winter's night in a St. Paul tavern, shyly trying the idea out on Greg when it was scarcely more than a vague, cigar-induced daydream.

What has followed is proof that a word of encouragement at the right moment can lead to a tremendous amount of labor.

Finally, I thank my parents, who transmitted to me their belief in the value of remembering and respecting the past. I hope that, in some small way, this book does both.

The Special Feeling We Had

It was June 1944. Dorothy had just turned twenty. She and her friend Lois were sitting at a picnic table in Whitewater State Park in southeastern Minnesota.

They sat at the table with their chins in their hands, watching the long shadows of an early summer evening spread across the grape-green valley. It was one of those achingly lovely June days.

The two young women were the only people in the park. But shortly after the sun dipped behind the bluffs and the river ceased to glisten, they heard voices. Boys' voices. Singing.

Dorothy can't remember just what she and Lois were talking about when the singing started. But she figures it had something to do with the war—or with something they would do "after the war."

"You thought about the war all the time," Dorothy says. "It was constantly in the newspaper and on the movie newsreels and on the radio. They were always giving us battle results, though I don't think they always gave us the bad news. And you knew so many boys over there."

Two winters earlier, Dorothy and Lois had traveled to La Crosse, Wisconsin, for a weekend shopping trip. On Sunday afternoon, they'd gone to a ballroom called the Avalon, where there was a dance for the soldiers stationed at nearby Camp McCoy. At the dance, Dorothy met a soldier named Jim, from Arkansas. Soon Lois met a soldier named Joe. By the time Jim and Joe shipped out to Ireland in the fall of 1943, they had "a kind of understanding" with Dorothy and Lois.

The summer of 1944 was a quiet one in Minnesota. So many young men by then were overseas, and so many other people had gone to Chicago or Washington or California to work in defense plants or war offices. Dorothy and Lois had stayed home in Winona because they had good jobs as secretaries.

They'd come out to Whitewater State Park and had rented a cabin for their one-week vacation. They were the only renters that week. They hiked and swam and sunbathed, and had hardly seen anyone in days. They had no idea where the strange singing could be coming from.

"At first it was very quiet, way off in the distance," Dorothy remembers. "But it kept getting closer, and the closer it got, the more beautiful it was. All these boys' voices in harmony, and they could really sing. It was down in the river valley below the bluffs, and it echoed from the hills. Just unbelievably beautiful.

"And then we saw them turn off the road and come down into the park. A big bunch of men, fifty or sixty. And they came down the valley, marching in formation, singing a marching song. And by then we could tell they were singing in German."

It was America's third summer at war. But that June, everything had changed. D-Day had finally come just a few weeks earlier. "Things looked different after D-Day," Dorothy says. "Better, because we'd invaded. But worse, too, because so many more American boys were in the thick of it.

"I knew Jim had to be in that thing, because that's what they'd gone over there for. But it was a long time before I got a letter, and then they couldn't tell you much

Dorothy Walters and Jim Tice at the Wisconsin Dells in the summer of 1943. In the war years, millions of American servicemen like Jim shipped out for duty in Europe and the Pacific, fortified by "an understanding" they had reached with a young lady back home, often after a hurried romance. Photograph courtesy of Dorothy Youso.

except that they were alive. Those letters were censored. He might have mentioned that they were in France, but I guess that was no big secret to the Germans by then.

"I don't think we ever thought about losing the war. You worried about losing a lot of men, but we weren't going to lose the *war*. Everybody was so committed. There wasn't any of this feeling that we didn't belong over there, or any uncertainty. None of that.

"It was a special time. You young people can't know the special feeling we had. In spite of how bad it all was, you really had a good feeling about this country. And in a way, for a young person who didn't have to go over there, I guess it was an exciting time.

"We hated the Germans, sure. We hated what they were doing. They'd started this whole terrible thing. At that time we didn't know about the concentration camps, but even then you'd begun to think that Hitler was maybe a little bit crazy. But, you know, I had a lot of friends who had German nationality. Lois was full-blooded German."

It took Dorothy and Lois a moment to realize that the singers marching toward them were prisoners of war. All of the singers were wearing green-brown fatigues, and the men walking alongside were wearing side arms. The prisoners, it turned out, were housed in the Civilian Conservation Corps camp across the road from the park.

"They came right toward us, right past us, heading for the beach to take a swim, singing all the way. We thoroughly enjoyed it. Those voices, swelling through those hills—and it was one of those long June days, you know. It was really thrilling. And it was nice to see we treated prisoners so well. I mean, here they were, going for a swim, in a spot we'd come to for vacation. There just wasn't much to get upset about.

"But they were young. Some couldn't have been more than fifteen. I couldn't believe they were so young.

"They marched right past us and hardly looked. Some of them looked at us with a kind of blank expression and then turned away. But two of them, two of the youngest ones, looked right at us, hard, and spit on the ground. They didn't spit at us, just down at the ground. Just to show us. And then we watched them cross the bridge and march down to the beach.

"That spitting wasn't very nice. You knew how much they hated you. We hated them for what their country was doing, but they hated us, too, maybe more. It seemed ungrateful. Here they were, being treated so well, but they didn't want to leave any doubt that all they had for you was contempt.

Lois Butenhoff (later Logelin), Jim, and Dorothy in 1946. Photograph courtesy of Dorothy Youso.

"You couldn't really blame them, of course. We knew that they'd been brainwashed from little kids on. Those younger ones had been just babies when Hitler came in. But still, it wasn't a very good feeling to know there were people who hated you so.

"But even with the spitting, it was something kind of nice. Nice and not nice at the same time—like a lot of things then. But we got a look at real people. You sort of lost sight of the fact that these Nazis, these soldiers, weren't strange creatures in uniforms and helmets, but just people. Just like we are. It sort of brought that home. I remember it fondly."

Jim survived Omaha Beach, the liberation of France, the Battle of the Bulge, and the final assault on the Reich. In later years he only rarely, and only when pressured, told combat stories—stories about wading ashore through blood-pink surf with body parts floating in the foam. But he, too, described those years as a special time, a time of purpose and unity. A time when things were nice and not nice all at once.

Dorothy and Jim, my parents, married in 1946.

Minnesota's
Twentieth Century

The Dawn of the Twentieth Century, 1901

Journalism is history in a hurry, written before all the facts are in.
But history, for its part, often feels like dull journalism. Facts are plentiful, but people are missing.

How the past *felt*—how it sounded and tasted and smelled: All that is dead as limestone.

Minnesota's Twentieth Century is an expedition in search of living history. The quest began for me with my mother's story of encountering German prisoners of war beside a southern Minnesota stream on a tender June evening. The ironic images haunted me from the first time Dorothy told me about them, when I was a teenager. They had by then already haunted her for decades.

There is something in that simple memory of Dorothy's that captures alive the "special feeling" of the World War II years—the pungent mixtures of beauty and ugliness, sorrow and inspiration; the improbable fates and meetings that global chaos arranged; the reminder that Dickens was right in thinking the best of times and the worst of times can be one and the same.

Dorothy's story convinced me that many Minnesotans must have personal memories that put flesh on the bones of history. It suggested that ordinary people whose lives have been touched by extraordinary events have a precious and perishable treasure to share with those who come after them.

Such true-life time travelers know not only the facts of the past, but also its moods and sensations. They know how it felt.

This conviction that humble, personal memories of Minnesotans are a storehouse of historical truths urged me to action as the close of the twentieth century approached. The "people of the century"—the famous, infamous, and influential—seemed sure to be remembered in an inevitable torrent of reflections on the life-transforming epoch. But would stories like Dorothy's be preserved—stories about the beautiful singing of boyish Nazis?

I decided at least a few of them would be.

The fashionable approach to history today often downplays the past's great events, and famous heroes and villains, on the theory that these have long been allowed to overshadow the everyday reality of life for multitudes of humble and often oppressed people. Anthropological history reigns in many quarters, focusing on the customs and lifestyles of the obscure, especially in minority cultures.

In one sense, *Minnesota's Twentieth Century* may seem to echo this modern microhistory theme. Most of its tales describe the lives of average Minnesotans. But the reader will soon notice that the twentieth century's legendary events make many appearances—that the book resides at the intersection of the mundane and the momentous. Though the traditional landmarks of mainstream history are far from the whole story of the past, they remain the chapters that contributed most to

A turn-of-the-century image captures St. Paul workmen, a stylish Summit Avenue lady, a carriage, and a streetcar passing by the lavish mansion of steamboat and railroad tycoon Norman Kittson. A monument to the astonishing overnight wealth the new industrial age could produce, the towered landmark was built in 1884 at the corner of Selby and Summit Avenues. It was razed just twenty-one years later, in 1905, to make way for a still more imposing edifice, the St. Paul Cathedral. *St. Paul Pioneer Press* file photo.

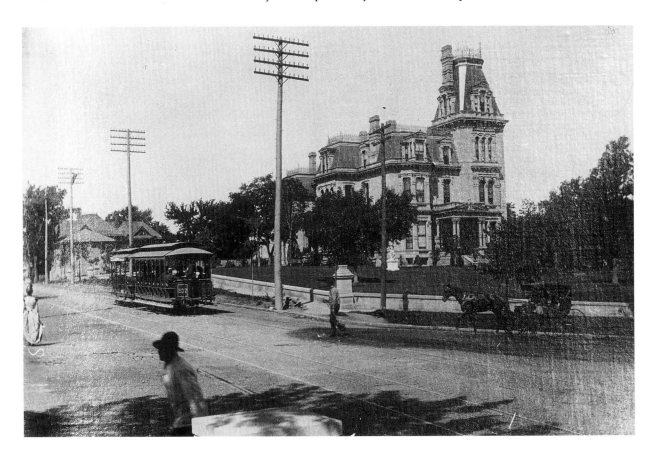

	1900	Today
Population of Minnesota	1.75 million	4.66 million
Twin Cities metro population	570,000	2.69 million
Percent of metro population in suburbs	36%	77%
Percent of Minnesota population in metro area	33%	58%
Farm population as percent of U.S. total	41.9%	1.9%
Percent of Minnesota residents foreign born	28.9%	2.6%
Life expectancy at birth (U.S.)	47.3 years	76.3 years
Infant deaths per 1,000 (U.S.)	162.4	8.4
Annual murder rate per 100,000 (U.S.)	1.2	6.8
Per capita gross national product, in 1992 dollars	$4,650	$25,588
Percent of high-school graduates among adults (U.S.)	6.4%	81.7%
Average hours worked weekly, U.S. manufacturing	59.1	41.6
Telephone main lines per 1,000 population (U.S.)	17.6	590
Miles of paved roads in Minnesota	67 (1906)	54,193

Sources: U.S. Bureau of the Census, Population Census, 1900 and 1990, *Statistical Abstract* and *Historical Statistics.* Minnesota Departments of Public Safety and Transportation. The "Today" column shows the most recent figures available at time of writing.

shaping the present in which we live. They are the stories contemporary readers naturally find most engaging, and most need to understand.

Minnesota's Twentieth Century, then, is a scrapbook of memories, portraying the grand sweep of history as the background of real lives. It is not a comprehensive narrative of the twentieth century, nor is it an attempt to broadly interpret the meaning and lessons of the modern age. If the book has an agenda, it is to recognize the durability of human dignity and the significance of individual actions in all the odd, touching, tragic, and heroic circumstances the twentieth century contrived for our neighbors.

The focus here is on personal encounters with the historic—Minnesotans' adventures, triumphs, and heartaches while residing in the exotic realm known as the past, the almost forgotten birthplace of the present.

The Fin de Siècle Spirit

What kind of place was the past? What kind of people were Minnesotans as the twentieth century dawned?

It helps to know that Minnesota, like most of the Western world, celebrated the start of the twentieth century on Tuesday, January 1, 1901—not a year earlier, at the more psychologically affecting moment when the "1800s" gave way to the "1900s."

A spirited public debate over when the century should officially turn had raged for decades. The year 1901 prevailed for nearly all official welcomes to the twentieth century because it was the more logical choice. Nobody, the reasoning went, counts to one hundred starting at zero and ending at ninety-nine. Thus, 1900 was the last year of the nineteenth century; 1901, the first year of the twentieth.

People revered logic at the end of the nineteenth century. The age was passionately rational and scientific, proud of its recent technological and economic breakthroughs.

Today, strict rationality seems less compelling, and the year 2000 has been widely accepted as the first of the twenty-first century. The psychological potency of that millennial number proved irresistible. It's also emblematic of our age that the modern hype and marketing machine couldn't wait a whole year to celebrate once-in-a-millennium markdowns and end-of-the-century sell-athons.

Our predecessors in 1900 were inspired and preoccupied by the impending change of the centuries. The evocative French phrase *fin de siècle* was coined in the 1880s to convey a widespread, unsettled mood during the "end of the century" period, a volatile blend of dark anxiety and boundless optimism.

The *St. Paul Pioneer Press* of the time was typical of newspaper boosterism in

In the early years of the twentieth century, it required a country outing to reach the intersection of Mississippi River Boulevard and Marshall Avenue in St. Paul, now near the center of the urban area. In this photograph, a family motors in that vicinity about 1912. Early twentieth-century Minnesotans were quite certain the nineteenth century's material progress would never be surpassed. *St. Paul Pioneer Press* file photo.

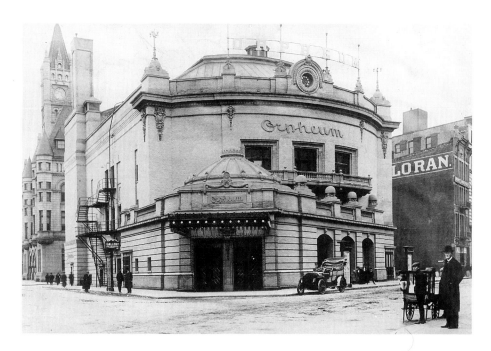

Opened in 1906, the Orpheum Theater in downtown St. Paul was one of the Midwest's premier vaudeville houses until its demolition in 1939. Sarah Bernhardt, Eddie Cantor, Al Jolson, W. C. Fields, Lionel Barrymore, and many other big names of the era played there. Behind the theater, notice Landmark Center (then the courthouse), which still stands. *St. Paul Pioneer Press* file photo.

expressing mostly the optimism. On January 1, 1901, the paper's editorial page urged readers to look forward to the certain progress of the twentieth century, leaving behind "habitual glorification of the Nineteenth Century." Yet the paper observed that "so much has already been accomplished in the way of purely material development that in this direction future progress may not be as striking."

Some tolerably "striking" material developments still lay in the future—modern automobiles and airplanes, radio and television, computers and organ transplants, space travel and cloning, to name a few. Yet the editorialist of 1901 was probably right that daily human existence had been more fundamentally transformed by the innovations of the nineteenth century.

"Not probably in the Twentieth Century," the editorial continued, "will the world be again so startled as it was by the adaptation of steam power to the purposes of manufactures and transportation, and by the 'chaining of the lightning' to the telegraph, the telephone and the trolley."

Railroads, steamships, engine-powered machinery, electric lights, and instantaneous communications had freed nineteenth-century humanity from ancient tyrannies of distance, darkness, and dependence on muscle power. A miraculous revolution soon followed in the productivity of factories and farms.

The volume of ready-to-wear ("store-bought") clothing made in the United States doubled between 1890 and 1900. Food production soared 40 percent from 1899 to 1905.

Minnesota was a fast-changing frontier economic powerhouse at the turn of the century. In 1900, the state ranked among the two or three leading centers in the world for the production of flour, lumber, and iron ore.

"We are living in the rapids of the stream of time," said one fin de siècle writer, describing a sensation of dizzying social and economic change that lasted the whole of the twentieth century. From the beginning, not everyone has been pleased with where the rapids seem to be sweeping humankind.

The late nineteenth century had introduced the industrial corporation. Appearing as abruptly as the steam engine and electricity, corporate industrialism changed society just as much. Never had there been such concentrations of private yet impersonal economic power. Never had the old, rural, homespun culture, with its moralistic view of life and strict but secure web of social obligations, seemed so endangered by urbanization, mobility, and economic ambition.

Science, for all its blessings, had introduced disturbing new ideas such as evolution and Freudian psychology—ideas that suggested hidden, animalistic motives behind human conduct. Old beliefs in free will and moral responsibility seemed threatened.

Industrialization caused cities to grow rapidly while the countryside lost population. A new class of landless, urban wageworkers formed and grew restless. Economically dependent and poorly paid, the laboring class was tempted by a sudden abundance of consumer goods and galled by the swaggering opulence of the new rich in what Mark Twain called "the Gilded Age."

Ignatius Donnelly was a radical reformer, incendiary orator, best-selling crackpot author, and Minnesota's most colorful nineteenth-century politician. He embodied the anxiety felt by many farmers and workers as a new urban, industrial culture arose, destroying many of the certainties of the old rural, homespun society. Photograph by John Collier; used by permission of the Minnesota Historical Society.

Tramps and Millionaires

A society of "tramps and millionaires" is what Ignatius Donnelly called it. Donnelly was perhaps Minnesota's best-known nineteenth-century politician. Yet the legislator, lieutenant governor, congressman, and vice-presidential candidate was most successful as the author of quirky, pseudoscientific books about the lost city of Atlantis and the true authorship of Shakespeare's plays. In all his roles, Donnelly was a flamboyant prophet of the anxiety that warred with optimism at the end of the nineteenth century.

Donnelly stood at the radical agrarian fringe of the great political movement of his day. "Progressive" reformers would eventually enact, in a flurry between 1900 and 1920, the first effective child-labor laws and antitrust laws, food-safety regulations, workers' compensation, the income tax, women's suffrage, and Prohibition.

Donnelly had proposed much of that and more decades earlier. He also offered predictions about the approaching twentieth century—predictions not quite so rosy as those of the *Pioneer Press*. In a best-selling novel of 1890, *Caesar's Column*,

Donnelly foretold the collapse of civilization in 1988. Society's ruin would be brought about through the extreme concentration of wealth in an all-powerful industrial dictatorship. This ruthless plutocracy would try to safeguard its position by encouraging debilitating indulgence in sex and all other appetites among the slavish hordes of "tramps."

What could save civilization from tyranny and moral rot? "Government," says the hero of Donnelly's novel. "Government . . . is the key to the future of the human race."

By the early twentieth century, stronger, nobler government seemed essential to most Americans and their leaders, from Republicans such as Theodore Roosevelt to Democrats such as Woodrow Wilson. From business regulation to Prohibition, moral reform through good government was the aim of all Progressive initiatives.

Today's social conservatives and economic liberals (who no longer agree about much) both have roots in Progressivism's desire to limit the damage to society's morals and institutions while negotiating the rapids of technological and economic change.

Minnesota's Twentieth Century may help readers judge whether the optimism or anxiety of 1900 has been more fully vindicated. What's certain is that both have had their moments, and that the hopes, fears, and debates of the twentieth century's dawning live on in our time.

Ignatius Donnelly died with his century. He succumbed to a heart attack shortly after midnight—on January 1, 1901.

In 1890, Ignatius Donnelly's best-selling futuristic novel, *Caesar's Column,* predicted the violent destruction of civilization in 1988.

Edward Gottschalk, as pictured in the *St. Paul Dispatch,*
was a gloomy drifter whose brutal crimes and jailhouse
suicide outraged St. Paul in 1905. Photograph from
Minnesota Historical Society microfilm.

The Gottschalk and Williams Murder Cases, 1905

As the twenty-first century begins, Minnesota is one of only twelve American states that do not allow the death penalty for first-degree murder.

Most states lacking capital punishment share Minnesota's moderate crime rate, its low-density, ethnically homogeneous population, and its tradition of social reform politics.

It may have been inevitable that Minnesota would abandon the death penalty during the idealistic Progressive Era of the early twentieth century. But the movement to abolish hanging gained momentum from a wave of shocking events in St. Paul.

Two gruesome double murders within two months, two botched executions, and an unabashed attack on newspapers' freedom to report such official bungling seemed finally to persuade Minnesotans that the death penalty was intrinsically uncivilized and undemocratic.

Even today, the story, which follows, is not altogether unconvincing.

A Butchered Butcher

The ordeal began on the chilled afternoon of Saturday, February 19, 1905. Just after the lunch hour, the still-warm corpse of Christian Schindeldecker was discovered in the back room of his ramshackle butcher shop at 523 West Seventh Street.

The butcher's mutilated body almost resembled his merchandise. He had been insanely hacked to death with one of his own meat cleavers, his head all but severed from his shoulders. Robbery was the evident motive.

For a week there were no solid leads to what newspapers quickly dubbed the worst crime in St. Paul's history. The city then offered a one-thousand-dollar reward for information, an immense sum at the time, and within one day police arrested Edward Gottschalk, a gloomy, thirty-three-year-old itinerant fisherman and tinsmith.

Police Chief John J. O'Connor announced a day later that his department was seeking a second suspect, who remained at large. This was Joseph Hartmann, Gottschalk's twenty-two-year-old frequent companion.

The search for Hartmann forged a bit of the legend of the storied police chief. O'Connor was then just beginning his three-decade reign as St. Paul's chief magistrate. He would become famous for controlling crime by negotiating deals with gangsters.

Taking personal charge of the Gottschalk case, O'Connor quickly concluded that the suspect had also slain Hartmann, his nervous young accomplice. The chief further deduced from sundry clues the approximate whereabouts of Hartmann's body.

By mid-March, O'Connor had deputies dragging the Mississippi River near Pike Island in Minneapolis. On March 17, they retrieved Joseph Hartmann's body. The skull was crushed and weights had been tied to the feet to sink the corpse.

With St. Paul's "worst crime" brilliantly solved, the city relaxed. But not for long.

Mortal Passion

In *Murder in Minnesota,* a classic of regional popular history first published in 1962, Walter Trennary immortalized the story that was to traumatize St. Paul all over again that spring of 1905. It is the story of William Williams, the last person legally executed in Minnesota.

A retired lawyer, history buff, and onetime president of the Minnesota Historical Society, Trennary says he wrote his entertaining crime anthology because he'd grown "tired of stories about missionaries and heroes and the good people. I wanted to show Minnesota has had an equal number of sons of bitches."

The "dreadful affair" that led to Williams's dreadful hanging was inspired, Trennary wrote, by "the mortal passion of love, which takes so many forms." Williams was a twenty-seven-year-old English immigrant. Like Gottschalk, he was described as a moody drifter.

In 1903, Williams met a fourteen-year-old St. Paul boy, Johnny Keller, while both were hospitalized. Soon a romantic attachment grew between the two. Several times the boy went off with Williams to distant cities, much to the predictable dismay and outrage of Johnny's parents.

By April 1905, the Kellers had persuaded Johnny to break off his relationship with Williams. The older man couldn't stand it. On the evening of April 12, less than two months after the Schindeldecker murder, Williams arrived at the Kellers' St. Paul apartment, quarreled with Johnny and his mother, and shot both dead.

Pictured in 1997, Walter Trennary, former president of the Minnesota Historical Society and author of *Murder in Minnesota,* immortalized the story of William Williams. Photograph by Joe Rossi for the *St. Paul Pioneer Press.*

Crime records were not uniformly or reliably kept in the early years of the century. It's not possible to precisely compare the local prevalence of murder then and now. But we can safely imagine that back-to-back double murders were a rare and appalling sensation in the St. Paul of 1905. That year, the estimated national murder rate was about one-fourth what it is today.

The *Pioneer Press* on May 11 deemed the day's scheduled proceedings before District Judge Olin B. Lewis "the most unique in the history of the state." First, Edward Gottschalk, who had by then pleaded guilty to murder, was to be sentenced to either hanging or life imprisonment. As soon as Gottschalk's future was planned, William Williams would go on trial for his life.

The *Pioneer Press* expressed its confidence in the "healthy effect" of executions. "Gottschalk should hang," the paper editorialized, belittling the "mawkish sentimentality" of anyone who doubted that "the gibbet is a fitting ornament [for] this sneaking, cowardly double murderer."

Judge Lewis entertained no doubts. He condemned Gottschalk to the gallows. Nine days later, he handed down the same grim sentence for Williams. The Englishman's insanity defense had persuaded neither jury nor judge.

A Great Deal of Gush

In its whole history, St. Paul had conducted only two hangings (although one was a double execution). Only twenty-five persons had been hanged under state law in all of Minnesota history. (This doesn't include the U.S. Army's execution of thirty-eight Indians in Mankato after the 1862 Dakota War.)

But in May 1905, Ramsey County Sheriff Anton Miesen found himself in the unfamiliar position of having not one but two guests at the county jail who had a date with the scaffold. The department's inexperience in hosting such festivities would soon become apparent.

Gottschalk and Williams faced death with differing temperaments. While Williams's "fortitude" impressed his guards and the newspapers, everyone seemed to detect cowardice in Gottschalk.

"He will break down" and "make a scene" and have to "be carried" to the scaffold, Gottschalk's jailers predicted to the *St. Paul Dispatch*. The vicious killer moaned piteously in his sleep, they reported.

Far away in Illinois, Gottschalk's father was also fretting about his wayward son's backbone. In a letter cruelly turned over to the *Dispatch*, the father issued "a pathetic plea for [Gottschalk] to be brave in the final test and not bring further disgrace upon his family by meeting his punishment like a craven."

Gottschalk fulfilled observers' low expectations. On July 19, 1905, despite

orders for a strict "suicide watch," the prisoner was left alone. Gottschalk quickly fashioned a rope with cloth fragments from his mattress and "robbed the gallows," as the *Dispatch* put it, hanging himself in his cell.

Sheriff Miesen fired the derelict guard, but he suffered most of the blame himself for what the *Dispatch* indignantly called the "tragedy" of Gottschalk's "third crime, self-slaughter."

The community outrage reflected in the newspapers over Gottschalk's do-it-yourself lynching, two weeks prior to his scheduled departure, seems almost inexplicable a century later. It's clear only that Gottschalk's suicide was yet another affront to the law, the community, and the killer's victims.

William Williams, for his part, won surprising admiration for his dignity in facing his punishment. The latter-day observer imagines that a homosexual who murdered his underage lover would have represented perfect, diabolical villainy to puritanical turn-of-the-century Minnesotans. Yet Williams's stoic bearing conferred on him something approaching nobility, at least in the newspapers.

Wrote Trennary: "A great deal of gush was poured over [Williams's] admittedly exemplary last days . . . his walk to the scaffold, his final words. . . . " Guards marveled at the condemned man's hearty appetite, sound sleep, good humor, and polite consideration for others as his end neared. The *Pioneer Press* report of Williams's hanging, on February 13, 1906, was headlined: "Displayed His Nerve to the Very Last."

But while Williams's performance was a big improvement on Gottschalk's, Sheriff Miesen again failed extravagantly. He got his man to the gallows this time, but in testing the machinery, he had overlooked what Trennary termed "the grim but elementary law of physics that if weight is applied to a rope and to a human neck, both will stretch."

The rope was six inches too long. Williams fell to the floor when the gallows trap was released. Two deputies had to grab the rope and hoist the victim a few inches off the floor. It took Williams fourteen minutes to strangle, and each minute of it was eloquently detailed in the newspapers. "Would the man never die?" implored the *Dispatch*.

It seemed that Sheriff Miesen would never get a murderer properly hanged in St. Paul. Governor John A. Johnson threatened to investigate the sheriff's botchery, but nothing came of it. In the following November's election, Miesen was soundly defeated in a reelection bid.

An Unwholesome Effect

Defenders of the death penalty knew disastrous publicity when they saw it. Within days of the Williams fiasco, a committee appointed by something called the Law and Order League called upon the Ramsey County Attorney. The committee directed the prosecutor's attention to a state statute known as the John Day Smith Law. They demanded that it be used to prosecute various St. Paul newspapers.

The Smith law had been passed in 1889, expressly to spare the public distasteful death penalty spectacles. It required that condemned prisoners be hanged in the wee hours of the morning, inside a jailhouse, and that no newspaper reporters be among the witnesses. The law also prohibited newspapers from publishing any detailed accounts of executions.

This severe, and today unthinkable, restriction on press freedom had from the first been universally defied by Minnesota newspapers, which routinely lavished breathless prose on hangings. The *Pioneer Press* openly ridiculed what it called Minnesota's "midnight assassination law."

In fact, the Smith statute had never been enforced against a Minnesota newspaper before the Williams hanging. But, then, no earlier hanging had produced such a story.

The *Pioneer Press* was prosecuted, and the constitutionality of the Smith law's censorship provision was challenged before the Minnesota Supreme Court in February 1907. The high court could see no problem whatever with the law, even though its "evident purpose . . . was to surround the execution of criminals with as much secrecy as possible, in order to avoid exciting an unwholesome effect on the public mind." In essence, the court ruled that newspapers had no constitutional right to publish anything the legislature considered "detrimental to public morals."

While this judgment was breathtakingly contemptuous of press freedom, the penalty for breaking the midnight assassination law was trivial—a twenty-five-dollar fine. Before and after the Williams case, early twentieth-century newspapers were considerably more free in practice than in theory.

Nonetheless, St. Paul's busybody newspapers were humbled. Gottschalk and Williams were dead. Autopsies of both men revealed what doctors called "criminal brains," rather resembling the brains of "wily animals."

But amid all the carnage, Minnesota's death penalty, too, seems to have been mortally wounded. Trennary wrote that capital punishment "was never really popular" in Minnesota. Judges had long looked for excuses not to impose it, and governors routinely commuted death sentences. After the ugliness of 1905–6, death penalty opponents seem to have been "jolted into action."

Extravagant media coverage of sensational events is not a new development. On the day of William Williams's hanging, the *St. Paul Dispatch* published this elaborate visual guide to the event, featuring photos of the crime scene, the killer, and the sheriff, along with a chart showing Williams's route to the gallows. After the botched execution, the papers grew even more breathless. From Minnesota Historical Society microfilm.

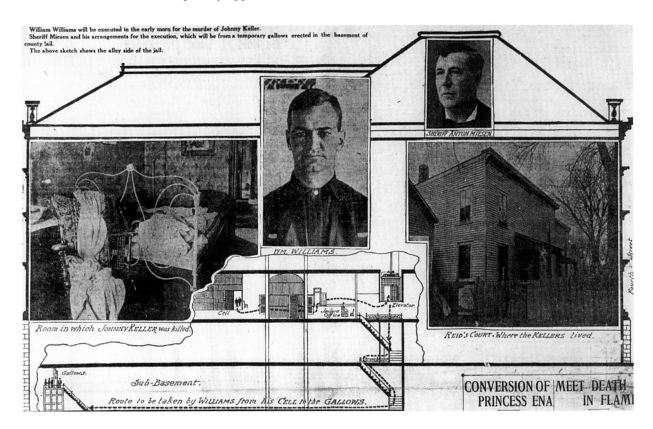

William Williams will be executed in the early morn for the murder of Johnny Keller.
Sheriff Miesen and his arrangements for the execution, which will be from a temporary gallows erected in the basement of county jail.
The above sketch shows the alley side of the jail:

WM. WILLIAMS.

SHERIFF ANTON MIESEN.

Room in which JOHNNY KELLER was killed.

REID'S COURT. Where the KELLERS lived.

Gallows.

Sub-Basement.

Route to be taken by WILLIAMS from his CELL to the GALLOWS.

CONVERSION OF
PRINCESS ENA

MEET DEATH
IN FLAM[

What we know is that William Williams was the last person legally executed in the state. The Progressive reform movement was gaining strength, with compassion for and rehabilitation of the wayward among its central themes.

In 1909, state representative George MacKenzie of Gaylord, a former prosecutor, took up the abolition of hanging as his personal crusade in the Minnesota legislature. Several Progressive governors refused to sign any more death warrants. In 1911, the legislature, with Governor Adolph Eberhart's support, outlawed capital punishment in Minnesota. Its restoration has never been seriously attempted.

By the end, the St. Paul newspapers seemed to see the death penalty as an unexciting, secondary issue. They described hanging's abolition in Minnesota on May 19, 1911, as a minor achievement in a mostly failed legislative session.

This parade through downtown New Ulm in September 1917 saluted draftees. Following a similar parade in July of that year, city leaders had spoken out against the war and the draft, triggering charges of disloyalty. Photograph courtesy of the Minnesota Historical Society.

The World War I
Loyalty Crusade, 1917

"We always have bands in New Ulm," says Ted Fritsche.

Fritsche remembers the high-stepping music of a brass ensemble ringing through the Minnesota River valley on the mellow midsummer's evening of July 25, 1917. It was the day of New Ulm's most memorable and painful event of the twentieth century.

In the cool of late afternoon, a spirited parade of draft-age men marched through the prosperous center of the German American enclave. The parade route ended at Turner Park, where a crowd of some eight thousand waited to hear New Ulm's leading citizens deliver speeches about America's recent entry into the Great War.

Unlike so much oratory in that age of bombastic patriotism, the New Ulm speeches did not denounce the wickedness of America's enemies, or laud the nobility of her cause. New Ulm's leaders rose to question the wisdom of America's war effort, to voice doubts about the constitutionality of the draft, and to promise efforts to win exemptions from combat for New Ulm's sons.

The speakers, Fritsche says, "never dreamed they had done anything that could be construed as being illegal or wrong. Under free speech, they had a right to speak up."

But in 1917, freedom of speech was under attack in Minnesota, and all across America. A coercive campaign to stamp out "disloyalty" and silence dissent swept the nation that summer.

Conservative scholar Robert Nisbet called the World War I loyalty crusade "the most complete thought control ever exercised on Americans." Soon after July 25,

Lois and Theodore Fritsche at their New Ulm home in 1998. Photograph by Craig Borck for the *St. Paul Pioneer Press*.

thought control was exercised in New Ulm, securing that small city's rueful place in history as the most prominent victim of Minnesota's notorious experiment in political repression—the Commission of Public Safety.

Fritsche was ten years old in 1917. World War I and its patriotic hysteria changed his young life.

It changed politics and society even more, in Minnesota and beyond.

Flesh and Blood

Theodore Roosevelt Fritsche was born in New Ulm in 1906, the youngest of six children. It was his father's idea to name the boy after America's popular president. Dr. Louis A. Fritsche, a Democrat, admired the Republican Roosevelt's "Progressive" efforts to limit the power of industrial monopolies and to conserve natural resources.

Reformist politics ran as deep in Fritsche's family as its roots ran in New Ulm. Grandparents on both sides of his family had been among the town's founders. They had come to America with a wave of German immigrants who had fled a widespread 1848 revolution in Europe and had begun to settle in Minnesota by the 1850s.

Fritsche's grandfather on his mother's side, Wilhelm Pfaender, led a large group of German "Turners" to the new community of New Ulm in 1856. The

Turners were a socialistic and anticlerical fraternal society that put great stock in physical fitness and athletics ("Turner" refers to a penchant for gymnastics). The Turner heritage remains important in New Ulm today.

Fritsche's grandparents on his father's side were also in New Ulm from its earliest days. His father was a babe in arms when the town came under attack during the 1862 Dakota War. That was the first time New Ulm had been near the center of a sprawling Minnesota conflict.

Louis Fritsche grew up and became a doctor, completing surgical studies in Berlin, Germany. Back in New Ulm, while practicing medicine and raising his family, his political interests led him to serve as city coroner and as a school board member before being elected mayor in 1912. That same year, Americans elected as president Democrat Woodrow Wilson, another champion of the era's bipartisan Progressive movement.

Two years later, World War I broke out in Europe, pitting Germany and

The Fritsche family at its New Ulm home, about 1910. Clockwise from front: Theodore Roosevelt Fritsche, Dr. Louis A. Fritsche, Carl J. Fritsche, William H. Fritsche, Albert Fritsche, Elisa Fritsche (later Bond), Louise Fritsche (later Menzel), Amahia Pfaender Fritsche (Mrs. Louis A.). The four sons became doctors, as have several grandsons and a granddaughter of Louis Fritsche. Photograph courtesy of Theodore Fritsche.

Austria-Hungary against Britain, France, and Russia. At first Americans, almost universally, wanted no part of what was seen as a free-for-all among arrogant old-world monarchies.

But slowly the isolationist sentiment waned. Sympathies for England among old-stock Americans combined with outrage over Germany's submarine warfare and with the Progressive Era's faith that America could reform the world as well as itself. In 1916, Ted Fritsche remembers, his father reluctantly voted against Wilson's reelection. Mayor Fritsche no longer believed the president's promise to keep America out of the war.

Wilson was reelected. Within months, the worst nightmare of many New Ulm citizens came to pass. America was at war with their own homeland, their own flesh and blood.

All Necessary Power

In *Watchdog of Loyalty,* his comprehensive study of the Minnesota Commission of Public Safety, historian Carl Chrislock explains that the World War I crackdown on "disloyalty" was in some ways a fatal culmination of Progressive ideology.

The Commission of Public Safety was given "all necessary power" to stamp out disloyalty in Minnesota and enhance the state's contribution to the war effort. Clockwise from front: C. H. March, Thomas Cashman, Anton Weiss, Henry Libby, Governor Joseph Burnquist, Attorney General Clifford Hilton, Ambrose Tighe (legal counsel), and John McGee. Photograph courtesy of the Minnesota Historical Society.

Beginning in about 1900, Progressives in both major parties had enacted America's first extensive business regulations and political reforms and had in general favored "increased use of government to solve social problems," Chrislock wrote. This faith in vigorous government "led them easily to the belief that a nation's right of self-preservation (in wartime) transcended constitutional limitations on governmental power."

In April 1917, soon after America declared war on Germany, the Minnesota legislature, following ferocious debate, created the Minnesota Commission of Public Safety. This remarkable body, chaired and appointed by the governor, was given "all necessary power" to maintain order and enhance Minnesota's contribution to the war effort.

Technically limited by the state and federal constitutions, the commission essentially wielded all the authority of state government during the eighteen months of its active existence. Dominated by representatives of the Twin Cities business community, the commission used its sweeping authority with gusto, not only to root out "disloyalty," but to combat labor unionism and agrarian activism as well.

The commission dispatched detectives throughout Minnesota to investigate people and organizations suspected of disloyalty. It regulated food prices and the liquor trade, imposing prohibition in some parts of the state. It banned union organizing and intervened on the side of management in a bitter Twin Cities streetcar strike. It created a "Home Guard" of some eight thousand troops to back up its decrees.

The commission served as a virtual campaign committee for Republican Governor Joseph Burnquist in his 1918 reelection bid. It turned a blind eye toward frequent mob harassment of his opponents. It interrogated and intimidated Minnesotans who declined to purchase Liberty Bonds to finance the war effort.

Although few other states established wartime tribunals with so many powers, the survival of free speech "unhappily, was not prolonged" anywhere in America, in the words of journalist H. L. Mencken. Many state laws and a federal statute flatly criminalized "seditious" speech. Outspoken critics of the government were jailed. Many observed that Wilson's war "to make the world safe for democracy" had made democracy unsafe in America.

During the war and on into the "red scare" of its immediate aftermath, Mencken denounced "Wilson and his brigades of informers, spies, volunteer detectives, perjurers and complaisant judges. . . . The liberty of the citizen has pretty well vanished in America. In two or three years, if the thing goes on, every third American will be a spy upon his fellow citizens."

The repressive spirit of the era had, besides the passions of wartime, two main

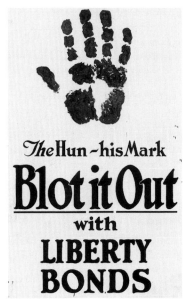

Belligerent anti-German sentiment swept America during World War I, as reflected in these Liberty Bond posters. *St. Paul Pioneer Press* **file photos.**

causes. America was traumatized in the early twentieth century by deep and emotional economic conflicts among workers, farmers, and business interests. It was "the nearest this country has ever come to a strong socialist movement," according to historian Nisbet.

Business leaders were horrified by radical political movements such as the International Workers of the World and the Non-Partisan League, a political coalition of farmers and laborers in Minnesota and North Dakota. The communist revolution in Russia in 1917 enflamed such fears and increased the determination of business interests to use the loyalty crusade to block trends toward unionization and socialism.

America also was crowded with new immigrants. In 1905, no less than 70 percent of Minnesotans were either foreign born or had foreign-born parents. Concern was widespread that newcomers might be less than wholeheartedly devoted to America's war aims or to its political and economic systems.

The Great War era had some parallels with the Vietnam period half a century later. In the 1960s, dissent about a war again mixed explosively with broader disagreements about American life. The difference is that in the earlier period, protest was effectively stifled in an all-out effort to promote national unity.

"Rarely," Nisbet says, "has the sense of national community been stronger than it was in America during the Great War. . . . [But] with these gains came distinct losses in constitutional birthright."

Not least in New Ulm.

Hog-wild

The evening of July 25 was cloudless and pleasant, Ted Fritsche remembers. A "tremendous crowd" filled Turner Park as Fritsche's father rose to address the throng.

Mayor Fritsche told the gathering that the purpose of the meeting was not "to cause any disaffection of the draft law." He cautioned the speakers who would follow him "to be careful about what they said," Fritsche remembers. Then he promised that New Ulm's leaders would petition Congress "not to force those drafted to fight in Europe against their will."

New Ulm was Minnesota's most German community. In 1905, the city, together with surrounding Brown County, was home to more than thirteen thousand first- and second-generation German Americans. Many had parents, siblings, and cousins still in the homeland. German was commonly spoken in New Ulm homes and taught in schools. The local "Irish kids," Fritsche recalls, "could rattle off German as well as we could."

Many New Ulm residents, Fritsche says, "had left Germany because they didn't like it over there. But they had warm feelings for that country. They didn't want to fight their own relatives."

Louis A. Fritsche, pictured here in 1929, was ousted as mayor of New Ulm in 1917. The Minnesota Commission of Public Safety accused him of disloyalty to America's cause in World War I. Photograph courtesy of Theodore Fritsche.

Following Mayor Fritsche to the platform was Albert Pfaender, Ted Fritsche's beloved uncle and New Ulm's city attorney. He told the audience that in his opinion the war was not supported by most Americans, and that it was unconstitutional to draft men for overseas combat. Only volunteers, he said, could properly be sent into combat on foreign soil.

Still, Pfaender urged young men to obey the law while their elders appealed to Congress for a combat exemption for German Americans. Other speakers offered similar sentiments, and the meeting broke up.

Within weeks, the "illegal character" of the "pro-German propaganda" disseminated by New Ulm's leaders was being decried by the Commission of Public Safety and by newspaper editorialists across Minnesota. One newspaper memorably regretted "that the Sioux did not do a better job at New Ulm fifty-five years ago."

In August, Governor Burnquist used the commission's authority to suspend Mayor Fritsche and City Attorney Pfaender from office. Letters arrived at the Fritsche home saying New Ulm officials "should be lined up against a wall and shot."

Fritsche remembers a day when an agent of the commission arrived to search their home for rationed food items, reducing his mother to tears with interrogation about "an old box of flour that had been on the shelf for years."

"People were hog-wild at the time," Fritsche says. "It's almost unbelievable that otherwise normal people could be so wrought up by the war hysteria that the right of free speech was completely squelched."

Before the year was out, the commission formally deposed New Ulm's Mayor Louis Fritsche and City Attorney Albert Pfaender. It then forced the board of Martin Luther College in New Ulm to fire President Adolph Ackerman, who had also spoken at the July 25 meeting. A newspaper editor who had spoken was later briefly jailed.

The Brown County medical and legal societies were pressured to expel Fritsche and Pfaender. When they refused, the county societies were ousted from the state organizations.

"My father was very humiliated," Fritsche says, "but never really bitter. He was a levelheaded man. He understood mob psychology and knew people could get carried away with themselves under duress.

"Me? I didn't think it was right."

Wrenching Nationalism

After the war, the reputations of Louis Fritsche and Albert Pfaender fared better than the reputation of the Commission of Public Safety.

In 1920, Fritsche's father ran again for mayor of New Ulm. He was returned to office by a two-to-one margin. In later years, Albert Pfaender became a regent of the University of Minnesota.

The commission's heavy-handed reign became a powerful political symbol, helping to build the left-leaning Farmer-Labor Party in Minnesota. Louis Fritsche became one of the new party's founders.

In the 1920s and 1930s, the Farmer-Labor Party scored major victories and established a durable bipartisan liberal tradition in Minnesota politics. Carl Chrislock says early Farmer-Labor success owed much to German American Minnesotans, a mostly conservative population estranged from the major parties for years after the loyalty campaign.

For America as a whole, the "wrenching nationalism" of World War I centralized American life more than any event except the Civil War, according to Robert Nisbet. A powerful and activist federal presence and the weakening of local governments and ethnic identities are among its lasting legacies.

During World War II, thousands of Japanese Americans were imprisoned as security risks. So were some German Americans. But there was in general less tension for German Americans than during the earlier conflict, largely because the war against Hitler had more universal support.

In Minnesota, liberal Republican Harold Stassen was governor when World War II broke out. He promised Ted Fritsche, a friend from college days, that "nothing like [the World War I crackdown] will happen as long as I'm governor."

Fritsche was by then a doctor, like his father, as were all three of his brothers. Four grandsons and a granddaughter of Louis Fritsche have become doctors as well.

Ted Fritsche practiced medicine in New Ulm for fifty-five years before retiring in 1984. In the 1950s, he again followed his father's footsteps by serving two terms as mayor. He still lives in New Ulm with Lois, his wife of sixty-two years.

New Ulm City Attorney Albert Pfaender, Ted Fritsche's uncle, was ousted along with Mayor Fritsche but later became a regent of the University of Minnesota. Photograph courtesy of Theodore Fritsche.

Masks, which offered no real protection, were commonly worn in public during the influenza pandemic. Here, nurses serve soup to the relatives of flu victims, often driven from their homes by the presence of the disease. Photograph used with permission of Corbis-Bettman.

The Influenza Pandemic, 1918

It was early November 1918. News from Europe brought rumors of an armistice. World War I would soon end, and a million American doughboys would come home.

But death marched across the autumn-brown Minnesota prairie that month as the guns fell silent in "the war to end all wars." Hattie Marier, a twenty-four-year-old farm wife and mother, was afraid.

Marier's eldest sister, Minnie, had influenza. It was a new, horrible strain—Spanish influenza, they called it. The epidemic blew across the countryside like a deadly gust of wind.

"Oh, the country was full of people I knew who were dying," Marier remembered. "And they died quickly. There was no help for them. There were more than the doctors could take care of."

Brutal epidemics were not exceptional in those days. Diphtheria, typhoid fever, and many other contagious plagues took their toll. One afternoon, Marier remembered, she watched as a neighboring farm family buried six children in their pasture, all lost in a single outbreak of diphtheria.

Influenza, too, killed its share, usually by turning into pneumonia in infants and the elderly. But in the fall of 1918, it was becoming clear that this new flu epidemic was something different, something terrible.

Without Parallel

Minnie was one isolated victim of a shocking global catastrophe. It could happen again.

Between the middle of 1918 and the middle of 1919, the worldwide Spanish influenza pandemic killed at least twenty-one million human beings—well over twice the number of combat deaths in the whole of World War I.

The Spanish flu had first appeared in America in spring 1918. The deadliest waves came that following fall and winter, amid the climactic events of the Great War.

Influenza slaughtered soldiers of all nations as viciously as machine guns. Troopships became floating horrors that greatly accelerated intercontinental transmission of the virus.

President Woodrow Wilson suffered a severe case of flu while in Paris in early 1919 negotiating the ill-fated Treaty of Versailles that ended World War I. Some historians believe the disease contributed to Wilson's failure to win a more conciliatory treaty from his allies, which might have prevented World War II.

All over the world, Spanish influenza savaged civilian populations. One-quarter of all Americans suffered bouts of flu. More than 600,000 Americans died, 10,000 of them Minnesotans. St. Paul saw more than 1,000 deaths; Minneapolis, more than 1,300. In New York City, 33,000 perished.

About 2 percent of the entire American Indian population was killed.

Lacking reliable statistics, official British colonial reports settled for describing the flu's carnage in poor, developing countries as being "without parallel in the history of disease."

Eight decades after the influenza pandemic, Hattie Marier had not forgotten its terrors. Marier is pictured here in 1997, at 102 years of age, at Birchwood Health Care Center in Forest Lake, Minnesota. She died during the spring of 1998. Photograph by Chris Polydoroff for the *St. Paul Pioneer Press*.

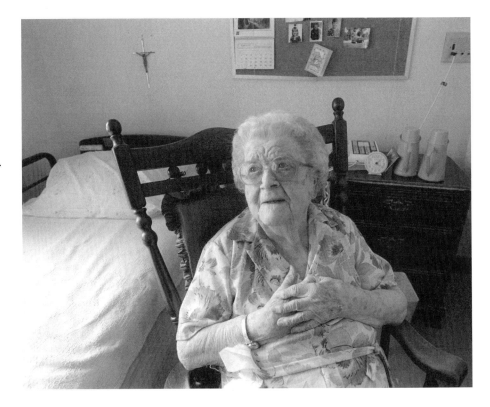

	1900	Today
Total annual death rate per 100,000 (U.S.)	1,720	880
U.S. annual death rate per 100,000 from:		
pneumonia and flu	202	31
tuberculosis	194	0.6
non-auto accidents	72.3	18.4
diphtheria	40.3	0
typhoid fever	31.3	0
heart disease	345	363
cancer	64	206
auto accidents	0	16.2
suicide	10.2	12.4
Maternal deaths, in Minnesota, per 10,000 live births	56.0 (1910)	0.8

Sources: U.S. Bureau of the Census, *Statistical Abstract of the United States, Historical Statistics of the United States,* National Center for Health Statistics, Minnesota Center for Health Statistics. The "Today" column shows the most recent figures available at time of writing.

Hard Living

The stricken Minnie had four children under age eight. Several brothers rushed over to handle farm chores for Minnie's husband. And even though the house was strictly quarantined, like all houses with flu that autumn, Marier's mother went to help nurse her eldest daughter.

Marier's was a close family of five sisters and four brothers. Their parents, Annie and Lazare Sevigny, were "real Frenchmen," Marier said, who had initially emigrated with their respective families to Quebec. There the couple met and married in 1882. Soon many members of both extended families moved on to Minnesota, helping establish one of the state's few French immigrant districts, near Forest Lake.

Marier was born August 22, 1894. She died in the spring of 1998, at 103 years of age.

"It was hard living in those days," Marier said of her turn-of-the-century girlhood on the farm. "People call them the good old days. Sure they were the good old days. But it wasn't fun all the time. It was work. We girls had to work like the boys to keep up the food."

On a summer's day in about 1910, Hattie Marier, at right, enjoys a smoke break with other girls of the Sevigny farm—her cousin Emily Bergeron (far left) and sisters Lenore and Libby. Photograph courtesy of Muriel Renard.

The Sevignys' eighty-acre farm yielded little cash to purchase store-bought goods. Annie and her daughters sewed nearly all the family's clothes. They milked cows and tended pigs, chickens, ducks, geese, turkeys, and horses. Daily they washed kerosene lamps—four for the barn and as many for the house—to ensure that they would work well into the black frontier night.

Often, Marier would wash the hand-operated milk separator, a laborious task she remembered with distaste nearly a century later. It was hauling water, from the outdoor pump to the stove to be heated, and back out to the shed where the separator was kept, that made the job hateful, she said. Hauling water for every purpose was a daily tyranny.

Machinery on the farm was limited. Sometimes the girls would ride horseback to pull a cultivator back and forth across sunbaked fields. "When you'd step off that horse," Marier said, "you were so dizzy you couldn't walk straight. The sun would beat on you so bad. Lots of times I had to vomit, the sun was so bright, the heat was so bad. But we had no choices.

"I'll tell you, we didn't need to find exercise. You didn't see kids like today, running down the streets in shorts. We were so anxious to get washed up and get to bed every day. And we had a hard time getting up the next morning."

More happily, Marier remembered reading in bed, upstairs in the farmhouse, along with her sisters. The girls would snuggle into their hay-stuffed mattresses beneath heavy quilts, with frost forming on the interior walls in winter, reading "storybooks" by the light of a kerosene lamp.

"That was our pleasure," Marier said. "We didn't have much pleasure."

The storybooks were passed from the girls of one farmhouse to the next. Mostly they read "love stories."

"We believed in that," Marier said.

With no education beyond eighth grade available, girls had few options to ponder. "All we had in mind," Marier said, "was that someday maybe I'll get older and get married. That was all we had to live on."

Marier recalls Minnie's early courtships. Minnie and a beau would sit in the front room, in company with another courting couple, while the younger children "would sit in the other room singing for them, to keep busy. They didn't want us in the living room with them." Suitors would often bring hard candies with little messages of admiration imprinted on them. "They weren't very rich boys," Marier said.

Kitchen dances brought married couples, courting couples, children, and the aged together. Nearly every week, Marier said, eight or nine farm families would gather at one house or another, haul the kitchen table outside to make room, and hold a raucous square dance. Marier's family had three harmonica players.

"Oh, and we had good times," Marier said. "That was the best. My dad was a jigger, a tap dancer. He'd sit there listening to the music, peppy music for square dancing, and his feet would start going and he just couldn't sit still. I'm the same way. When they play a good mouth organ, my feet are moving."

Already Gone

Hattie Marier had been married a year and a half when her sister Minnie fell ill with the awful flu of 1918. Hattie had married a builder, Clement Marier, in April 1917, the month America entered World War I.

"He had nothing and I had nothing, but we got married anyway," Marier said. A well-to-do farmer had hired Clement and gotten him exempted from the wartime draft. Marier had recently borne the first of four children.

Her mother returned from Minnie's bedside with the worst possible report. "She said, 'She's already gone.' Something in my sister's eyes warned mother that she was gone. She lived only three days."

How could flu, mere flu, kill healthy young adults so quickly and brutalize the world the way it did? Minnesota's former state epidemiologist Mike Osterholm explains that the 1918 flu virus was exceptionally "virulent" to begin with. It then underwent several sudden mutations in its structure. Such mutations can turn flu into a killer because its victims' immune systems have no antibodies to fight off the altered virus. Fatal pneumonia can rapidly develop.

Deadly flu pandemics struck again in 1957 and 1968, Osterholm says. In 1975–76, international health officials were horrified to detect outbreaks of the same flu virus that had caused the 1918 nightmare. A national immunization campaign vaccinated much of the American population against what was then called "swine flu." No major epidemic developed.

But Osterholm is emphatic that a 1918-style horror could be repeated. Unlike modern contagious killers such as AIDS, flu is easily passed from one victim to another through the air. Today's frenetic international travel means, Osterholm says, that a deadly flu pandemic could spread with supersonic speed.

And though modern doctors have drugs that physicians of 1918 lacked, germ resistance to drugs and the swiftness with which fatal flu can kill mean that the right bug could still bury millions.

The 1918 disaster did much to inspire development of professional public-health agencies across America. But the vast human tragedy of the pandemic has not been well remembered. Overshadowed by great events of war and peace, Spanish influenza has taken its historical place as merely an especially bad epidemic in an era of many epidemics.

Marier in 1942 with Pudgy beside the log house where she and Clement raised their family. Photograph courtesy of Muriel Renard.

The modern world can only hope never to see its kind again.

Marier took her baby boy with her when she went to pay respects to her dead sister. Typically, in that community, a corpse was laid out for visitation at home for several days. But no one was permitted to enter Minnie's house—so great was the danger of flu.

"They stood her up in her casket in the front-room window," Marier remembered. "We could walk by, on the outside, and visit her that way. I had never seen before somebody stood up like that. I wanted to see my sister. I took my baby because I had no one to leave him with.

"We couldn't even go to the burial. We couldn't even go to that. They buried her all by herself, with just her husband there."

The war was over. Minnie had died on Armistice Day, November 11, 1918.

Raids on bootleggers became routine news stories during Prohibition. Their frequency may have proven only that oceans of illegal alcohol were being manufactured—not that enforcement was particularly effective. Here, St. Paul officials confiscate illegal beer. *St. Paul Pioneer Press* file photo.

A LOT OF PREACHERS,

A LOT OF GANGSTERS

Prohibition, 1920

The sleek Cadillac touring car rumbled along dark, snow-covered St. Paul streets. At the wheel was Richard Thomas Hooton, a twenty-three-year-old chauffeur. By his side was his employer, wealthy businessman George M. Kenyon.

Tom Hooton drove carefully that January night. "Drivers had to be drivers in them days," he remembered. "You had to know how to get through mud and snow. There wasn't much plowing. You always carried chains just in case."

That night, there was no time for delay. Kenyon was riding up front because it was January 16, 1920. At midnight, Prohibition would take effect throughout the United States. The Cadillac's backseat was occupied.

Hooton told the story of his Prohibition-eve midnight ride, and of his decades-long career as a driver in St. Paul's posh Hill District at its aristocratic peak, in an oral history recorded in 1975. It is now in the Minnesota Historical Society's collection. Hooton died in 1981.

Pretty Fancy Baby Buggies

Hooton was born to Irish immigrant parents in Council Bluffs, Iowa, in 1897. When his father died in 1912, young Hooton moved with his mother to St. Paul and soon entered the opulent world of Summit Avenue and what were called the "merchant princes" of the city. His first job was delivering groceries in the Hill District by horse-drawn wagon.

"Summit is not the avenue it was, and it never will be again," Hooton said in 1975. "It was a rich man's street, and everybody who lived on it was well respected, too." In 1915, horses remained common on Summit, pulling not only delivery wagons but stylish carriages. Already, though, barns and carriage houses were being converted into garages and guest houses.

A colleague of Tom Hooton at the Blue and White Cab Company in the 1920s poses with his taxi on Summit Avenue. Cabbies were the principal retailers of moonshine liquor during Prohibition. *St. Paul Pioneer Press* file photo.

Novelist F. Scott Fitzgerald was growing up in the Summit neighborhood in those years. Rarely more generous than necessary to his hometown, he would describe Summit Avenue as "a museum of American architectural failures."

Certainly many of Summit's colossal Victorian mansions ("mausoleums," Fitzgerald called them) were almost comically ostentatious and ornate, with their cupolas, towers, and mazes of gables. They preserve to this day the conspicuous displays of wealth that were fashionable among turn-of-the-century aristocrats.

Yet, Hooton remembered the rich of his youth as unpretentious. Many were newly wealthy, self-made in the explosive economic boom of the late nineteenth century, tycoons of railroading, lumbering, land speculation, and industry.

"There wasn't any snobbishness," Hooton insisted, recalling how upper-crust debutantes would kid chauffeurs and other male servants about "stepping out" with them. Still, social classes were distinct, and so were classes within classes. "There were three classes of well-off," Hooton said. You could tell where a family belonged by which market delivered their groceries.

Later, when Hooton landed a job as chauffeur to the Kenyon family, he entered the upper strata of the servant class, which included such lesser figures as butlers, maids, cooks, laundresses, gardeners, and nursemaids.

In about 1918, the chauffeurs of the Hill District founded the Chauffeurs Club, above the Curling Club at Dale and Selby. Beyond providing a place for drivers to relax and socialize, the club helped out-of-work chauffeurs find employment. It also "laid down a few rules," Hooton said, about what kinds of menial work chauffeurs could and could not be required to do. "The beginning of a union is what it was," Hooton said.

The Kenyons were good employers. Hooton "had it easy." Daily he would drive George Kenyon to and from work at the railway- and construction-supply firm he owned, headquartered in the Pioneer Building in downtown St. Paul. The family lived in the Livingston Apartments at 442 Summit. Two days a week, Hooton would drive Mrs. Kenyon shopping and visiting. But on many other days, the Chauffeurs Club saw a lot of Tom Hooton. So did the Knights of Columbus gymnasium and swimming pool.

The Chauffeurs Club had about a hundred members. Hundreds of other servants lived and worked in the Summit neighborhood, creating a lively society.

Thursday night was maids' night off all along Summit. "Lake Phalen and Lake Como were pretty well populated on Thursday night," Hooton remembered. He kept a canoe of his own on Lake Phalen. Summit-area employers sponsored servants' balls several times a year and a servants' picnic every summer. In winter, ice skating, silent movies, and vaudeville shows were major amusements.

Hooton recalled the pleasures of watching Summit's nursemaids stroll the avenue on summer afternoons. "There were some beautiful girls pushing baby buggies down that avenue, I'll tell you. And they was pushing some pretty fancy baby buggies, too."

Members C. F. Zimmerman (left) and M. L. Ellsworth relax in the main lounge of the Minnesota State Chauffeurs Club, decked out for Christmas in 1929. The club was above the Curling Club at 470 Selby Avenue. Chauffeurs were the aristocrats within the servant class in St. Paul's swank Hill District. *St. Paul Pioneer Press* file photo.

A Couple of Shares

On the night Prohibition came in, no one could tell how effectively the radical new law would curtail bottled amusements. A nervous, carnival atmosphere prevailed across St. Paul, Hooton said. Many saloons stayed open all night and were "the busiest they'd ever been. Oh, they sold an awful lot of liquor that night."

But Hooton and his employer didn't linger; they had a mission.

As the "dry" years went by, it became clear that Prohibition was not being successfully or vigorously enforced. "There was more liquor during Prohibition than there was before," Hooton said. His impression was based on direct experience. "I drank my share," Hooton said. "Maybe I drank a couple of shares."

What's more, by the late '20s, Hooton was driving a cab and, like most cabdrivers of the time, he was "making more money selling moonshine than driving people around."

In the Prohibition era, as today, children made persuasive props for every political message. A repeal poster urged that children's security depended on restoring the legal liquor trade, while a float in a "dry" parade in St. Paul (opposite) warned that reopening saloons imperiled childhood purity. *St. Paul Pioneer Press* file photos.

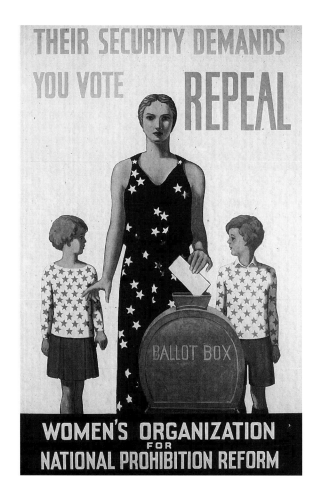

Hooton's view that Prohibition utterly failed to reduce drinking was not un-common during the dry years and has become almost universal in the decades since the repeal of the "noble experiment." The supposed spectacular failure of Prohi-bition is today widely and uncritically cited as irrefutable proof that all prohibitions must fail—that it is impossible to outlaw vice or "legislate morality."

Yet, some historians say Hooton was simply wrong. Alcohol consumption, their studies show, dropped by between one-third and two-thirds during Prohibi-tion, and did not return to pre-Prohibition levels until the 1970s (it has been de-clining anew since the 1980s). John Burnham, an Ohio State University historian, adds that the gangland crime and violence commonly blamed on Prohibition is often exaggerated.

Prohibition failed politically, revisionist scholars say, because it was unpopular with many Americans (who evidently thought it did interfere with their drinking) and because politicians longed for revenue from alcohol taxes, especially as the depression of the 1930s set in and other revenue sources dried up.

Nonetheless, there is no doubt that Prohibition was flagrantly disobeyed. Most of St. Paul's moonshine came from stills around Somerset, Wisconsin, Hooton said. Bootleggers there apparently "had a good understanding" with the authorities. Many others who "handled" booze had "good understandings," too. Hooton re-

Prohibition authorities delighted in showing off the results of their efforts. At right, St. Paul officials empty a cache of moonshine. Anoka County sheriff's deputies (facing page) display distilling equipment taken in a farm raid. *St. Paul Pioneer Press* file photos.

called a St. Paul tobacco shop from which customers routinely emerged carrying "pretty good-sized packages of tobacco." And there was the Sweet Shop ice-cream parlor, where "there was more spiked beer drunk than ice cream ate, I'll tell you that."

Hooton always kept a liquor bottle or two beneath the front seat of his cab, "where you could get it quick and break it." Customers could mix drinks with the moonshine or make "spiked beer" by adding moonshine to fortify the low-alcohol "near beer" that was legally marketed throughout Prohibition.

Hooton knew some bootleggers and major dealers who were arrested by federal authorities, but nobody bothered the cabdriver retailers, he said. "I'll tell you," he added, "crooked cops didn't just come in lately."

Jazz Age

Cabdrivers of the 1920s were brokers of every vice. Beyond selling booze, they directed fares to gambling opportunities in various St. Paul hotels and to brothels. For delivering what was called a "laundry load" to a house of prostitution, the cabbie would be paid half of the typical five-dollar fee for each trick—"more than the girl got," Hooton remembered.

"Yes, a cabdriver dealt with everything from preachers to gangsters," Hooton said. "And in them days, there was a lot of preachers and a lot of gangsters."

The Roaring '20s still lay ahead as Hooton and Kenyon ran their errands on the eve of Prohibition. Unsure how dry conditions might become, Kenyon was determined to save and stockpile the liquor supplies remaining at St. Paul's best private clubs, where he was a respected member.

"We had to go to the Elks Club and carry all the liquor out and put it in the backseat of the Cadillac," Hooton said. "And then the Athletic Club. Then we went and unloaded all that. The last place we went was the University Club up on the hill. The old man brought the liquor out from there himself. We had a tough time figuring out where we was going to put all that liquor."

Of the 1920s, Hooton said: "That's when Summit Avenue started to change." The costs of maintaining mansions and houses crowded with servants became too much even for some merchant princes. Mansions were subdivided and rented out. The servant population on the hill began to shrink.

The whole of American society seemed, to many, to change in the '20s. There arose a new modern spirit of moral freedom, of intoxication with life's pleasures, of disdain for the inhibitions and moral pretensions of the old order—of which Prohibition was the last desperate spasm. What was arriving was the free-living Jazz Age that Summit Avenue's own F. Scott Fitzgerald was to epitomize and immortalize.

On a cold January night, Tom Hooton drove George Kenyon's Cadillac touring car out of one era and into another.

The shocking scene in downtown Duluth, June 15, 1920. Issac McGhie, Elias Clayton, and Elmer Jackson were dead. Accused of rape, almost certainly falsely, the black circus workers were lynched in what was by many measures the worst crime in Minnesota history. Photograph courtesy of the Minnesota Historical Society.

The Duluth Lynchings, 1920

Michael Fedo first heard the story from his mother. He grew up in Duluth in the 1940s and 1950s. The story came from his mother's own childhood. It was not widely told.

By the 1970s, Fedo had become a college professor, eager to write books. He planned a historical novel that would include a version of the incident his mother had described—a lynch mob overwhelming police and hanging three black rape suspects from a light pole.

"I thought I should read something about it," Fedo says. "I assumed that somebody had to have written a book about it."

But nobody had. The more Fedo checked, the more he discovered that the Duluth lynching of 1920 was an orphaned episode of Minnesota's past, largely ignored in conventional state history texts.

Fedo soon had a new project. Relying on newspaper accounts, court records, state files, and interviews with aging and often reluctant witnesses, Fedo published *Trial by Mob* (originally titled *They Was Just Niggers*) in 1979.

The book has had a troubled career, with several bankrupt publishers and the ill-chosen first title diminishing its sales. Yet more than twenty years after its appearance, it remains the best known and most requested of Fedo's books.

Fedo has met some resentment over the years, from blacks as well as whites, for exhuming gruesome and unhealthy memories. Others have called him heroic for preserving unpopular but revealing truths about Minnesota's racial history. Fedo himself insists he is merely a writer who found a compelling story to tell.

Conflicting reactions to the tale that follows are understandable. It is a story that cannot help but shock and sadden contemporary Minnesotans, while leaving them a bit better informed about the origins of today's racial divisions.

Coon Rapids author Michael Fedo has met both praise and resentment for chronicling the Duluth lynching. Photograph by Joe Rossi for the *St. Paul Pioneer Press*.

An Incendiary Charge

In the early morning hours of Tuesday, June 15, 1920, a nineteen-year-old Duluth woman and her boyfriend reported a gang rape to police.

The woman and her beau, both white, said they had been confronted by six black workers from a traveling circus whose sideshow they had visited the night before. Holding the boyfriend at gunpoint, the assailants had taken turns raping the woman, or so the story went.

By nine o'clock that morning, evidence surfaced that the story might not be true. Duluth physician Dr. David Graham examined the alleged victim. He formed the immediate opinion, which he never changed, that whatever had happened to her, she had not been violently raped by six men.

But even if it would have mattered, the doctor's opinion was unknown to scores of angry young white men who, by lunchtime, were gathering in Duluth pool halls and on street corners. Rumors flew about the alleged crime. Big talkers vowed revenge against six blacks who were, by then, in custody at the downtown police station.

Duluth was a city primed to explode, according to Fedo. Like all America in 1920, the lakeside steel and shipping center of 100,000 (as large then as it is today) was sharply divided along economic lines. West Duluth's large and not-very-prosperous working class was bitter that the city's big U.S. Steel plant had begun importing low-wage black workers from the South, in what was seen as a union-busting maneuver.

The blue-collar ranks of West Duluth, where the alleged victim lived, were also filled with restless veterans of World War I. An unqualified horror for Europe, the Great War had been in many ways a splendid eighteen-month adventure for America.

Veterans, Fedo says, "had never been anywhere before. The Europeans treated them like heroes. They'd gotten a big parade when they got back. Many would have liked the war to have gone on a bit longer."

"How You Gonna Keep 'Em Down on the Farm after They've Seen Paree?" went a popular 1919 song. Returned to their drab, everyday grind, young veterans were hungry for another adventure, another cause, another fight.

"Rape," Fedo adds, "was an incendiary charge, then as now."

By late afternoon on June 15, swarms of grimly determined men wandered through downtown Duluth. Ringleaders prowled the streets in pickup trucks, rounding up volunteers.

But police did not believe warnings that a lynch mob was in the making.

Pythons and Rabbits

When Edward Nichols read an afternoon newspaper report of the allegation that black men had raped a white woman, he concluded at once that a lynching was likely.

Edward Nichols in army uniform in 1918. Nichols returned from France to his home in Duluth, where restless white veterans of World War I were enraged by racially charged allegations of rape in the summer of 1920, and were tempted to prove their heroism again. Photograph courtesy of Charles Nichols.

Nichols was a twenty-year-old black truck driver in Duluth. Decades later, he became an important source of information for Fedo, whose book uses the narrative of Nichols's fearful all-night vigil, revolver in hand, to dramatize the terror that gripped Duluth's tiny black community of about four hundred the night of June 15.

Nichols died in 1987. His son Charles, a retired educator in Brooklyn Center, explains that the idea of a racially motivated lynching in Duluth was more incredible to the city's whites than it was to its blacks.

The commonplace lynchings of African Americans in the nineteenth and early twentieth centuries were a horror that primarily plagued the southern United States. But blacks never doubted that it could happen anywhere.

"To people of color, lynching was a very practical, everyday occurrence at that time," Nichols says. "The networking in the black community was extensive. When something happened in Mississippi, it came as news to somebody in Duluth who was white, but it was old hat to somebody in Duluth who was black.

"So just as we know that pythons are going to eat rabbits, we knew that black

Edward Nichols (right) with his brothers Bob (left) and Bill, about 1920. Photograph courtesy of Charles Nichols.

folks were going to get lynched. The fact there was a lynching in Duluth was an oddity, but it wasn't something extraordinary."

Regardless of race, lynchings were always uncommon in Minnesota, though not unknown. Race relations were not unusually bad in Duluth. As everywhere in America in the first decades of the twentieth century, Duluth blacks were socially isolated and restricted to humble jobs as waiters, laborers, and domestic servants. In time, Edward Nichols would become notable in the Duluth black community as the owner of his own business, a tailoring and catering service.

Still, day-to-day relations among whites and blacks were peaceful, says Charles Nichols, who was born in 1924. "There was no sense I recall of foreboding or threats," he says.

But as afternoon gave way to a long June twilight the evening of the rape charges, the wrong combination of circumstances was about to summon the spirit of the python.

The Lynching Psychosis

At about seven o'clock, a fusillade of bricks and stones shattered most of the front windows of the Duluth police station. A mob numbering at least five thousand choked Superior Street, the city's main thoroughfare.

Sergeant Oscar Olson was in command at the station. As the mob and the threat of trouble had grown, Olson had mustered some twenty-five officers to protect the prisoners. But it was already too late to move the suspects to a safer location.

Soon after the brick throwing began, two respected Duluth judges hurried downtown and spoke to the crowd. Judge William Cant, who was, according to Fedo, "a sober man of frequently eloquent rhetoric" and "decidedly conservative philosophy," told the mob: "If you do this terrible thing, you will never live it down, and neither will Duluth."

For a time, the mood calmed. But soon shouts and taunts resumed as the mob swelled. Sergeant Olson gathered his shaken men, some of whom, Fedo wrote, were suffering "nervous diarrhea." Olson ordered the officers to "avoid shooting as long as you can," but "shoot if you have to."

Just after eight o'clock, the mob rushed the station. In the initial fighting, Olson led his men in aggressive countercharges, freely swinging their nightsticks and setting the attackers back on their heels.

But sometime before nine o'clock, a fateful order was issued by Commissioner of Public Safety William Murnian, Duluth's top law-enforcement officer. Police were not to use guns, or even clubs, against the mob. Murnian later told a reporter that he "would not want to see the blood of one white person shed for Negroes."

Fedo attributes Murnian's cowardice, in part, to his political support from, and sympathies for, the working-class men who dominated the mob.

Famed early twentieth-century journalist H. L. Mencken, a fierce critic of what he called America's "lynching psychosis," wrote, "The impulse to perform lynchings is present everywhere and at all times. But in order that it may lead to actual murder, there must be a preliminary collapse of police power, an antecedent breakdown in the orderly process of justice. Once that breakdown occurs, a lynching is imminent."

	1892	1900	1920	1930	1952
Whites lynched	69	9	8	1	0
Blacks lynched	161	106	53	20	0

A lynching is defined as the illegal killing of a person by a group acting under pretext of justice. Statistics include only victims identified as black or white. Estimates from 1882 to 1903 are that approximately four additional lynchings per year victimized Indians, Asians, or Hispanics. The year 1892 was the worst on record for lynchings in America, and 1952 was the first year that no lynchings were officially noted. *Source:* U.S. Bureau of the Census, *Historical Statistics of the United States.*

Murnian's order provided the ominous breakdown in Duluth. It is difficult to believe a lynching would have been completed had police continued to wield their clubs decisively or fired even a single shot at the mob's leaders.

Fedo's impression is that no more than a few score of rioters were spoiling for a serious fight with police.

Nothing to Do with God

Denied the use of clubs or guns, Sergeant Olson and his men turned fire hoses on the mob. Rioters cut some hoses and seized control of others. Injured by flying bricks and battered by water, officers slowly "lost their stomach for battle," Fedo wrote. "One by one, they dropped off their hose, until only Sergeant Olson remained."

In addition to Olson, one other Duluth officer, Lieutenant Edward Barber, was credited at the time, and by Fedo, with fully discharging his duty and battling the mob as best he could under Murnian's order.

Around ten o'clock, the mob broke through the station door. A hellish scene unfolded inside the squad room, flooded ankle-deep with water from the fire hoses and swarming wall to wall with hysterical rioters. Olson, Barber, and others climbed a stepladder in the center of the melee and vainly tried to reason with the mob as its leaders took hammers and saws to the cell-room door.

The horror of the six suspects waiting inside that cell room is neither possible nor pleasing to imagine. Little is known about the prisoners, except that they were simple men, mainly from the South. It is unknown whether any of the six had been involved in any way in whatever had transpired the night before behind the circus tents.

It is widely assumed that some kind of disagreeable encounter triggered the rape charges. Charles Nichols notes the theory that it may have been a prostitution transaction gone bad. Fedo says it could have been as simple as some blacks whistling at the young woman or discovering the couple in a sexual embrace.

Mob leaders conducted a grotesque parody of a trial once they'd surged into the cell room. Yet, the first victim the vigilantes dragged out into the street, Issac McGhie, had not even been suspected by police of participating in the alleged crime. He was being held only as a potential witness.

Bloodied and begging for his life, McGhie was marched a block from the jail to a light pole on Second Avenue from which a rope dangled. A last plea for sanity was offered by a priest, the Reverend William Powers. With the noose already around McGhie's neck, Father Powers fought his way forward and climbed several feet up the light pole.

"Men, you don't know this man is guilty," Powers cried. "In the name of God . . . I ask you to stop!"

"This has nothing to do with God," a man in the mob was heard to say.

Powers was pulled down from the pole, and McGhie was hoisted up, where he convulsed and died. Within minutes, two more victims, Elmer Jackson and Elias Clayton, followed him.

A car was pulled up to illuminate the grisly scene. A photo was taken, with mob members posing in a half circle around their handiwork.

The photo, made into a ghoulish postcard in the days after the lynching, was reproduced on the jacket of Fedo's book. One day, he says, a widow visited his father's Duluth home and took an unusual interest in the book, which was lying on a coffee table.

Pointing to one of the pictured lynchers, she whispered, "My goodness, that's Carl."

It was her deceased husband. She had never before heard of the incident.

A Little Spark of Justice

"The most atrocious crime in all our history has been committed," Judge Cant told a grand jury empaneled two days after the lynchings. "The great wrong to the victims can never be undone. The laws of God and man have been defiled . . . With righteous indignation . . . discover and punish the perpetrators."

Considering the multiple victims, the hundreds of coconspirators, the assault on the rule of law as well as on the dead, and the dereliction of duty by Murnian and some police, the Duluth lynching was arguably the worst crime in Minnesota history. It was widely denounced at the time, but not universally, and not, in some cases, without regrettable qualifications.

A *Pioneer Press* editorial took pains to condemn "lynch law," but used more space to speculate that the tragedy might never have occurred had capital punishment still been legal in Minnesota.

The notion was popular that Minnesota had gone soft on rapists after hanging was outlawed in 1911 (the penalty in 1920 was up to thirty years in prison). Fedo believes this idea helped fuel the mob's rage.

Yet, historian Walter Trennary, who researched Minnesota's history of hanging, is unaware of any case in which a rapist was ever executed under state law. The lynching psychosis overwhelmed facts.

National Guard troops, equipped with machine guns, took to Duluth's streets in the days following the lynching. Their commander publicly announced that no further prisoners would be molested "until the last soldier has been killed." Such resolve might have saved the day on June 15.

The grand jury indicted nineteen mob leaders on charges including murder. Three were convicted of mere rioting, while several others were acquitted. The prosecutions then stopped, as it became clear that juries were incapable of reaching consistent verdicts.

Two circus workers were tried for rape. One, Max Mason, was convicted on flimsy evidence. William Miller was acquitted after his fiery black attorney, Charles Scrutchin, pleaded with jurors to prove there remained "a little spark of justice burning." Judge Cant then dismissed charges against several additional blacks who had been accused.

Two investigations of the lynchings found Commissioner of Public Safety William Murnian guilty of "malfeasance in office" for forbidding police to repel the mob by whatever means necessary. Yet, he was reelected in 1921. Two years later, the lynching again became an issue in Murnian's reelection bid, and he was soundly defeated. He never again held public office.

Lieutenant Barber and Sergeant Olson remained on the Duluth police force. In 1941, Olson was shot and killed by a fleeing suspect.

In early 1925, after serving just four years of a thirty-year sentence, Max Mason was released from Stillwater State Prison. The reasons for this unusual decision were never publicly explained.

A Legacy of Distrust

When he was growing up in Duluth, Charles Nichols remembers, "Dad told us as much about [the lynching] as he wanted us to hear. He didn't want my brother and me to grow up angry and hating. . . . We were taught to look at the absurdity of it, how wasteful it was. How denigrating it was both to people of color and to people in the mob. There were a lot of guilty white folks walking around Duluth after that."

In 1991, seven decades after the crime, the long unidentified graves of the three lynching victims were finally properly marked in Duluth, in a ceremony Fedo attended.

Charles Nichols's father, Edward, managed his tailoring business in Duluth and served as an officer of the local NAACP until 1956. He then moved to the Twin Cities and worked as a building superintendent for St. Paul's Hallie Q. Brown–Martin Luther King Community Center.

Charles Nichols went into education, becoming the first black school administrator in Minnesota and serving as Minneapolis director of vocational education.

Retired educator Charles Nichols was taught to remember the "absurdity" and "waste" of the lynching when he was growing up in Duluth. Photograph by Joe Oden for the *St. Paul Pioneer Press.*

He was an adviser on educational issues to four Washington administrations and later went into the aviation construction business. In 1999, he was appointed chairman of the Metropolitan Airports Commission.

Nichols, like Fedo, agrees that the anger and alienation in parts of today's African American community are, in many ways, a legacy of a history tragically rich in atrocities like the Duluth lynchings.

Such stories may also help explain black cynicism about the integrity of the criminal justice system, the depth of which sometimes startles whites. America's polarized reaction to such events as the O. J. Simpson trial is less mystifying in the harsh light of past injustices.

"Racism is alive and well," adds Nichols, while also noting that race relations have improved enormously during his lifetime.

"We shouldn't forget this history," he adds. "I can't blame [today's whites] for that lynching. But I have to let my children know that this happened. The best defense against any of this sort of nonsense is education.

"The nonblack community has a responsibility to know that disgraceful thing happened, and to stop every instance of bigotry.

"History has taught us that bigotry doesn't pay."

Minnesota underground iron miners, about 1920. They worked like mules, Frank Hrvatin said, and these men show it. Photograph courtesy of the Iron Range Research Center, Chisholm, Minnesota.

The Milford Mine Disaster, 1924

At about 3:45 on the afternoon of February 5, 1924, Frank Hrvatin (pronounced her-VAH-tin) was pushing an ore car along a shaft of the underground Milford Mine.

The dark, cool, horizontal shaft, called a "drift," was about eight feet wide and eight feet high. It was heavily timbered on all sides for support. The drift lay 175 feet below ground on the Cuyuna Iron Range in north-central Minnesota.

Hrvatin was seventeen days short of his fifteenth birthday. He was a "dirt trammer," one of forty-eight miners at work on the afternoon shift. His job was to shovel loosened iron ore into a tram, a big steel wagon on wheels, and then push the load by hand down rail tracks laid along the drift.

Hrvatin had just dumped a load of ore down a transfer chute when he was hit, he said, by "a terrific wind." The powerful rush of warm air was "very, very, very odd for a mine that was so quiet and cool all the time. There wasn't supposed to be no wind. No way."

Hrvatin then "looked down the chute. And I seen water coming through on the level below us. It bounced up into the chute and dropped back down and rushed on. I said to my partner, Harry Hosford, 'Look at the water, Harry.'

"He said, 'Water, you're nuts.' And then he looked and said, 'Oh, my God! My God!'"

Frank Hrvatin died in 1976, just weeks after recording his story of the Milford Mine disaster in an oral history. It is now in the collection of the Iron Range Research Center in Chisholm, Minnesota.

More than a half century after the worst accident in Minnesota mining, Hrvatin's voice rose and cracked and his breaths came quickly as he remembered.

Electric lights went out throughout the mine. The unnatural gale kept extin-

A photograph taken at the Zenith mine on the Vermillion Range in 1911 gives a sense of the damp creepiness of early underground mining. *St. Paul Pioneer Press* file photo.

guishing the carbide gas lamps the miners wore on their hats, plunging them into absolute blackness. Frantically, they relit the lamps again and again as a liquid roar rose from the depths of the mine.

"Oh man, scared," Hrvatin said. "Don't tell me about scared."

A Way of Life

Underground iron miners rarely worried about the hazards of their work, according to Hrvatin. "It was a way of life," he said. "These were men who earned their living that way every day for years and years. If you let yourself worry about danger, you'd never go down in that shaft to begin with."

Mining was a way of life Hrvatin's parents had tried to leave behind. German-speaking immigrants from Austria, the elder Hrvatins were among many thousands of poor newcomers from eastern and southern Europe who journeyed to northern Minnesota around the turn of the century. The richest iron ore deposits in the world had been discovered there in the 1880s.

The Hrvatins settled in Chisholm, on the largest of Minnesota's iron ranges, the Mesabi. There, after working in the mines for a time, Hrvatin's father, Frank Sr., opened a saloon, while his mother, Frances, ran a boardinghouse for miners. A disastrous 1908 forest fire destroyed much of Chisholm, including the elder Hrvatins' business. Frank Sr. was forced back into the mines. Frank Jr. was born a year later, the second of nine children and the only son.

Hrvatin's father sought a fresh start on the Cuyuna Range, a newly discovered iron region near what is best known today as a popular resort district north of Brainerd. The deep-lying ore of the Cuyuna was often mined by underground methods. It was prized because the Cuyuna ore contained large concentrations of manganese, making it ideal for heavy, high-grade steel. Top-quality steel was consumed greedily during and after World War I.

In 1922, the elder Hrvatin went to work for the Milford Mine, by then the only underground Cuyuna mine still producing the best manganiferous ore. Owned by George H. Crosby, a mining magnate after whom the nearby town of Crosby was named, the Milford tapped a rich ore body that ran near Foley Lake.

Just how close to the lake the mine reached would soon become a question of considerable interest.

The eleven Hrvatins lived in Crosby, a typically drab company town of that era on the Iron Range. They had a five-room house on a one-acre lot. They kept a cow and a few pigs. Young Frank's eight sisters "idolized" him, the way he remembered

Minnesota miners prepare to be lowered into an underground mine. "If you let yourself worry about danger," Hrvatin said, "you'd never go down in that shaft to begin with." Photograph courtesy of the Iron Range Research Center, Chisholm, Minnesota.

it. Rich in such boyish pleasures as fishing, hunting, and brawling, Hrvatin had, he said, "as much fun as any kid in the country."

He didn't much care for school. In the fall of 1923, he joined his father in the Milford. There was no problem about the fourteen-year-old's age. "They never asked, if you were a strong boy," Hrvatin said.

Hrvatin earned $3.80 a day as a dirt trammer. His father, an experienced miner skilled in the underground blasting that loosened the soft red ore, earned $6.00 a day. They both "worked like mules," Hrvatin said. But with two paychecks coming in, the family "had just started to get on our feet real nice financially" as February 1924 arrived.

It was a boom time on Minnesota's Iron Range, a region whose economy has always experienced extreme cycles of prosperity and hardship. "Everybody needed steel like crazy," Hrvatin said. "Everything was working. They couldn't get the ore out of that mine fast enough."

Somethin's Wrong!

Hrvatin and his fellow miners couldn't get themselves out of that mine fast enough once they realized the Milford was filling with water and mud. "I'll tell you, I had superhuman strength," Hrvatin said. "Boy, did I go."

Along with five other miners at the 175-foot level, Hrvatin scrambled up a 40-foot manway to the 135-foot level. From there they were about two football-field lengths away from the vertical shaft and its ladder to the surface.

"We heard that water coming down the drift and felt that wind," Hrvatin said. "We didn't know if we were going to make it. We just ran and ran for our lives."

Several men who had a chance to survive failed to save themselves. A miner named George Butkovich had run from the far end of the mine, near the cave-in. "He was all in," Hrvatin said. "He couldn't make it. He died right there."

Two other miners, Valentine Cole and Mynar Graves, refused to believe the mine was flooding. "They turned and went the other way," Hrvatin said. "They walked right into death."

Cole and Graves apparently realized their mistake, but by then they couldn't outrun the flood. They were eventually found, still standing, only fifty feet from the main shaft, their arms wrapped around each other.

"The mud must have trapped them so they couldn't move their legs," Hrvatin said. "What could they do? They grabbed each other and said a prayer, I guess."

Sprinting and stumbling their way down six hundred feet of dark drift, Hrvatin and the others at last reached the vertical shaft. There, another miner, Emil Kainu, met them. He had climbed up from the pump room.

Said Hrvatin: "Kainu cried, 'What's the matter? Somethin's wrong! Somethin's wrong!' He was a Finn. One of the older men answered him: 'Save your breath and start climbing. We know what's wrong.'"

Bubbling, Bubbling, Bubbling

In fact, to this day, it's not possible to know with complete satisfaction exactly what went wrong in the Milford Mine that day.

An exhaustive official investigation was conducted that spring by a special panel appointed by Governor Jacob Preus. But the committee lacked subpoena power. This meant that all three hundred witnesses testified "voluntarily." It's natural to worry that voluntary witnesses might have held back criticism of their bosses for fear of retribution.

The committee concluded that the flooding of the Milford was an unavoidable "act of God," and that no one was to blame. The committee ruled that the mine was nowhere closer to Foley Lake than three hundred feet, a distance engineers were justified in considering safe.

Labor advocates and miners, including Frank Hrvatin, have always insisted that part of the Milford Mine reached under Foley Lake, an irresponsible risk inspired by mining company greed.

What isn't in doubt is that a cave-in occurred in the far reaches of the Milford Mine. Mud and water, perhaps from a swamp bordering Foley Lake, poured into the mine with horrible force and speed.

Of the forty-eight miners on the afternoon shift, most were working quite near the cave-in and had no chance of survival.

For the seven lucky men who reached the main shaft, survival depended on how fast they could climb 135 feet of wooden ladder. Their tomb was close behind, gaining on them.

"We were climbing that ladder as fast as we could go," Hrvatin said. But Matt Kangas, just above Hrvatin on the ladder, was an older man whose strength was failing.

"The water and mud caught us right in the shaft," Hrvatin said. "That's how fast it was coming in."

Hrvatin's partner, Harry Hosford, was the bottom man on the ladder. "He was in mud up to his hips!" Hrvatin said. "He shouted up, 'If you can't climb, get the hell out of the way and let somebody climb who can climb!'"

Hrvatin had to get Kangas moving. He pushed himself up between the old man's legs, boosting Kangas up the ladder as if giving a child a ride on his shoulders.

"He just hung on to the ladder with his hands," Hrvatin said, "and I carried his

"Main Street" at the Milford Mine property, February 5, 1924. Iron miners lived spartan lives, some in these cramped shacks on mine property itself. The Hrvatin family lived in a house in the nearby company town of Crosby. *St. Paul Pioneer Press* **file photo.**

weight. Harry Hosford kept on hollering, and the men kept struggling their very, very best."

Those seven men reached the surface, where their legs buckled and they collapsed as if they'd been shot. Alarm whistles were madly shrieking and, already, "people were crazy in that town," Hrvatin remembered. "They couldn't believe it."

It was obvious there would be no other survivors. Mud rose to within twenty feet of the top of the shaft, where Hrvatin watched it "bubbling, bubbling, bubbling."

He added: "I knew then I'd never see my dad no more. They were all dead."

The Milford Mine disaster killed forty-one men, leaving thirty-eight widows with ninety-six fatherless children. Workers' compensation, then in existence for only a decade, paid the widows up to twenty dollars a week for up to seven years. But that's about all the help they got.

Mining companies were unusually generous toward one another. They launched a heroic recovery effort, using equipment and workers donated from many firms on all the ranges. Month by month, they pumped out not only the mine but Foley Lake. It took from February to November to bring up all the bodies.

Shortly after that, mining of the Milford's rich ore resumed.

Hrvatin worked on the grisly recovery effort until his father's body was found in the middle of June. Then he quit. He was fifteen years old, and on his own.

Hrvatin worked in later years as a factory hand, a construction worker, a truck driver, and a ditchdigger. He married in 1933 and fathered five children.

At various times, Hrvatin even returned to underground mining, descending again down damp and narrow shafts with a carbide light on his hat. He worked in Montana mines as deep as five thousand feet.

"It didn't bother me," Hrvatin said of going back underground. "I was with my kind of people: miners."

At the time of Quentin Fairbanks's childhood, traditional techniques and structures were used at Red Lake fishing camps, such as this one in 1929. *St. Paul Pioneer Press* file photo.

Life on and off the Reservation

"I've worked all my life," Quentin Fairbanks says, "just to get back to what I had as a kid. I didn't know how good I had it.

"I didn't know how bad I had it, either, until somebody started telling me how poor I was."

In the 1930s and 1940s, Fairbanks grew up on the Red Lake Indian Reservation in north-central Minnesota. In those depression and war years, even more than today, the roughly 800,000-acre reservation, about the size of Rhode Island, was among the most physically and culturally isolated Indian enclaves in the United States.

This land of "the lost tribe," as Fairbanks remembers it, was also a barely blemished wilderness of water and woods, and of broad wetlands "black with ducks." Reservation children were enveloped in a comfortable and welcoming ethnic community, whose equality dulled the pain of its poverty. It was the kind of place, Fairbanks remembers, "where a boy had a dog and not a worry in the world."

As a young man, Fairbanks felt compelled to leave the reservation in search of economic opportunity. For three decades he lived, worked, and succeeded in a larger society that he found in many ways discontented and poor, for all its affluence, in ways his threadbare childhood had been rich. In 1988, Fairbanks returned to work for his tribe and rediscover the "peace of mind" that comes, he says, "when you're with your own."

Fairbanks has lived out both of the dominant American Indian experiences of the twentieth century—the attempt to preserve distinct cultures on reservations, and the attempt to adapt and prosper within the irresistible alien society that surrounds them. Yet his search for a way to do both is, in another sense, purely personal, Fairbanks says.

Quentin Fairbanks strolls the still undeveloped shore of Red Lake. In his youth, the remote and independent reservation was "just another country," Fairbanks says. Photograph by Joe Oden for the *St. Paul Pioneer Press*.

"I cannot speak for other Indians and they cannot speak for me," he says. "That's not the Indian way."

Allotment

In the late nineteenth century, white Americans concluded that previous policies toward American Indians had to be abandoned. Those policies had mainly consisted of confiscating Indian land and pushing tribes progressively farther west, onto isolated reservations where, in theory, they could live as they pleased.

Indians were a small and powerless population. Today, somewhat surprisingly, Indians make up about twice the percentage of Minnesota's total population that they did in 1900.

By the 1880s, the frontier was being rapidly settled, and the growing nation's appetite for farmland, timber, and other resources was so voracious that even remote and often undesirable reservation lands were lusted after. Many white Americans also believed that the only hope of a decent future for Indians was for them to discard their tribal identities and traditional ways to become "Christian farmers."

What followed was a policy of forced assimilation, pursued through varying strategies, and with varying degrees of intensity, through most of the next century. The first and most dramatic strategy was called "allotment."

In a series of laws before and after the turn of the century, Congress decreed that reservation lands should be broken up into separate plots, or allotments, for individual Indians. Nearly every tribe in the United States eventually went along with some version of this arrangement, and the results were often tragic. Indians unwisely sold their allotments, or were swindled out of them. Tribal lands shrunk to small fractions of the original reservations, which became "checkerboards" of Indian-owned and white-owned property.

There were few exceptions to this pattern, but Red Lake was one of those few. From the 1860s forward, leaders of the Red Lake Ojibwe (Chippewa) band adamantly refused to sell or allot tribal land or to be consolidated with the other Ojibwe bands in Minnesota. "We want the reservation we now select to last ourselves and our children forever," said May-dway-gwa-no-nind ("He that is spoken to") during treaty negotiations in 1889.

The Red Lake tribe was compelled to cede millions of acres in north-central Minnesota. But it retained its large, contiguous reservation intact, nearly surrounding Upper and Lower Red Lakes. It is one of only two "closed" (all tribal-owned) reservations remaining in the United States.

It was into this strong-willed "nation within a nation" that Quentin Fairbanks was born in 1932. The reservation's extensive natural resources, particularly Red Lake fish and abundant game and timber, had meant Red Lake Indians "weren't starving," Fairbanks says. They could afford to refuse allotment.

Still, independence "was very hard on Red Lake." Because of its remoteness and unusual closed status, Red Lake received even less government assistance and was even less attractive for private investment than other reservations. "It was just another country," Fairbanks says.

"The best time we had on the reservation was during the depression," Fairbanks adds. Various emergency New Deal initiatives brought employment programs to Red Lake.

Poverty, nonetheless, was universal. Tar-paper shacks were the most common form of housing. Fairbanks's family was a little better off than some. His father was a laborer and his mother ran a small general store. They had a three-room log-and-frame home heated by a woodstove. Fairbanks daily hauled all the family's water (about eight pails a day) from a nearby spring.

Plumbing and septic systems were virtually unknown on the reservation, except in the homes of Bureau of Indian Affairs (BIA) officials who governed Red Lake as a kind of occupied territory. Fairbanks remembers the BIA superintendent, an ex-cavalry man who strode about in high boots running a whipcord through his hands.

But there was nothing harsh about BIA government, Fairbanks says. "They treated us like colonials," he adds. "They treated everybody like children." The BIA ran a sawmill and a fish-processing plant that were the main sources of employment.

Diseases that were scourges everywhere in those years, particularly tuberculosis, took an especially appalling toll on the reservation, where poor diet and hard living conditions weakened resistance. "Whole families would get wiped out," Fairbanks says.

Fishing by Hand

"If everybody around you is rich, you're not rich," Fairbanks says. "If everybody around you is poor, you're not poor. You're just as rich as the next man.

"Our isolation was an advantage in many ways," Fairbanks says of his youth on the reservation. "Nobody had anything more than anybody else. Indians can handle that. Whites can't handle it. That's why communism failed. Everybody in the white race wants to be better than the next person, and that's what drives our economy."

Red Lake boys in 1966, much like the children of Fairbanks's era, pose with a fine catch of perch and walleye. *St. Paul Pioneer Press* **file photo.**

If equality helped ease the hardships of Red Lake's poverty, so, for Fairbanks, did close relationships with family. He especially admired his grandfather, a "good gentle man," Fairbanks says. "He was never a hero, but he was a man."

Fairbanks's grandfather, born at the end of the nineteenth century, possessed uncanny traditional skills that the boy struggled to learn. His grandfather would lie down on the bank of a stream and place one hand in the water. There he would lie for a long while, still as a log, until you almost suspected he was asleep. Then suddenly he would pull his hand out of the water holding a fish.

If you hold still enough, Fairbanks explains, a fish will enter a cupped hand, attracted by its warmth. Fairbanks learned this much of his grandfather's technique. But he could never manage to close his hand slowly enough to trap the fish before it sensed its peril and swam away.

Fairbanks also remembers his grandfather's good-humored humility. Often, he says, when his grandfather would complete some task, he'd say, "Well, that's good enough for the Indians." Fairbanks would protest that his grandfather, too, was an Indian, and he'd answer: "Yeah, I know, but it's good enough for me."

Working, fishing, and hunting with elders, gathering maple sap, and navigating vast Red Lake aboard homemade rafts were among the simple pleasures of a reservation childhood. Fairbanks recalls spending whole days watching wildlife—thousands of migrating trumpeter swans, eagles, moose, bear, beavers, minks.

Among the more unusual childhood activities Fairbanks remembers was pushing old tires down the streets. "Everybody did it," he says. "It was good exercise, and we didn't have many bikes. So you'd push a tire over to your friend's house."

Today, children face a more complex, competitive life, Fairbanks says. They have more, but they also want more, and if anything they feel a greater sense of deprivation, he suggests. "I can't say our [reservation] children are better off today," he says. "But what children are better off today?"

Fairbanks attended elementary school at the St. Mary's Benedictine mission, a fixture at Red Lake from the 1850s until today. For many decades, St. Mary's operated boarding schools for Indian children, another prominent and often condemned feature of assimilation policy. Indian families were long forced to turn their children over to government or church boarding schools. "They basically stole the children," Fairbanks says, "and tried to take away all their Indian habits and ways."

Fairbanks never attended the Red Lake boarding school, which was winding down its operations by the time he started school. But he went to day school at St. Mary's and has only warm memories of that experience. "They did more for the Red Lake Indians than any organization I can think of," he says of the mission's nuns and priests. "They educated us, they clothed some of us, they fed us, and sacrificed

The dormitory at the Red Lake boarding school, 1925. Government and mission boarding schools, designed to distance Indian children from their traditional cultures, were among the often-condemned strategies of "assimilation" policy. Quentin Fairbanks attended a mission day school and has warm memories of the experience. *St. Paul Pioneer Press* file photo.

their lives for the betterment of the Indians. They taught me discipline. They taught me how to work. They were the foundation of my life."

Suffering a speech impediment, young Fairbanks would stay after school each day with Sister Delores, who used the venerable pebbles-in-the-mouth technique to help the boy master pronunciation. "This is how I learned to speak," Fairbanks says.

Blending In

The assimilation policy "succeeded" to the extent that large numbers of Indians left reservations throughout much of the twentieth century, generally to take up residence in cities. Many have continued to battle poverty, unemployment, and social problems, but many others have quietly prospered. Today about three-quarters of Minnesota Indians live off reservations.

Since World War I, Indians have been well represented in the armed forces. Fairbanks left Red Lake for the Marine Corps in the early 1950s. He served as a frontline air-support observer in Korea and saw extensive action.

The military was his first experience of the outside world, and he says it was good for him. "Everybody was always bitching about the food," he remembers. "I thought it was the best food I'd ever eaten. I had a bed to sleep in. I kept ten dollars a month for myself and sent the rest home. That was good living."

After a short time working back on the reservation and then getting a college education in Duluth, Fairbanks faced a difficult choice. "Do I want to go back to the reservation and try to make a living with that economy? Or should I put up with some things I don't agree with in white society in order to survive?"

He chose to engage the wider world. He served with the Minnesota State Patrol in Duluth for fourteen years, then bought a restaurant, a hardware store, and a sporting goods shop. He became an example of the Indians he says people rarely notice. "You don't see the Indian who gets up and goes to work every day, the teacher who's Indian or the nurse or doctor who takes care of you. They're Indian but they blend in.

"Indians have to learn that they can go and celebrate their holidays, but on Monday morning they better get up and go to work. Lots of Indians are doing that, but you don't notice. They're not sitting on a street corner drinking a bottle of beer, but they'd get more attention if they did."

A decade ago, Fairbanks reversed his youthful choice and decided to follow his yearning for a "quiet, peaceful life." He accepted a job with the Red Lake tribe as

Red Lake girls at their boarding school, 1923. *St. Paul Pioneer Press* **file photo.**

director of several property maintenance and elderly assistance programs and bought a home not far outside the reservation boundaries.

He shrugs off suggestions that he's motivated by a selfless desire to serve his people. "You just want to come back to your home," he says.

No Rush

"What race or nationality was ever civilized within a hundred years?" Fairbanks asks. He does so to call attention to the jarring transition American Indians have been called upon to make. The twentieth century's technological and cultural revolutions have been disorienting enough for mainstream American society, let alone for Indian societies that enjoyed no gradual preparation for the modern age.

Fairbanks's return to Red Lake came amid significant changes in Indian life and American attitudes toward Indians. For several decades, the idea of assimilation has been giving way to a reinvigorated call for tribal sovereignty and self-government on reservations, for the preservation of a distinct Indian culture. In a sense, Red Lake's militant spirit of independence has become the norm.

The arrival of casino gambling on reservations, and the financial resources it brings, has also transformed reality and perceptions. At remote and populous Red Lake—with some six thousand reservation residents, according to Fairbanks—casino revenues are not producing wealth, but they are creating jobs and funding services like those Fairbanks manages.

Still, serious problems persist, not least poverty and unemployment. In recent years, Red Lake has had to close fishing on its big lakes, which are depopulated after decades of heavy commercial harvests under both government and tribal management. As at other reservations, there are complaints of injustice and corruption in tribal government.

Fairbanks, acting as a kind of unofficial economic development agent, is laboring to attract private business to the reservation, to take advantage of its workforce, natural resources, and tourism attractions. Through his own programs, Fairbanks is having success, he says, in teaching basic work habits to long-unemployed and supposedly "unemployable" people.

Eager as he is to improve the economy of Red Lake, Fairbanks says he is pleased to be reconnected to what he describes as a humbler and less anxious society. Education and enhanced cooperation with the outside world will continue to bring progress to Red Lake, he says.

But "Indians are never in a rush to do anything," Fairbanks adds. "It's not their way. They like to work with everything in harmony."

White America is wrong, he suggests, to think its restless mindset is inherently superior. "In Korea," Fairbanks recalls, "if they put up a gate that opened the wrong way five hundred years ago, that gate will open the wrong way until the end of time. Americans are always changing everything."

Despite all the painful change forced upon them, "most Indians are content with themselves," Fairbanks says. "They're happy with what they are and what they do."

That goes for Fairbanks, too, now that he's gotten back to what he had as a kid.

Thousands of dust storms, "blizzards of dirt" as Phyllis Brantl remembers them, rolled across America's prairies during the 1930s, including this monster in 1935. Photograph from AP/Wide World Photos; reprinted with permission.

The Great Depression, 1934

They had closed up the drafty old farmhouse as best they could.

Ten-year-old Phyllis Hills; her sister, Byrte (pronounced "birdie"); and their mother, Elizabeth, had even padded the front door with quilts. "It didn't close real good," Phyllis remembers.

They had no radio. They couldn't afford one. So they took turns playing the piano. They sang and talked and read Bible verses and tried not to listen.

But all day long, trucks and wagons rumbled past the house on their way to the far end of the pasture. All day long, from where the trucks were headed, the Hills women heard what they didn't want to hear.

"We couldn't help waiting to hear it, you know," Phyllis explains. She says she will hear that sound forever.

At the dumping grounds beyond the pasture, farmers from the area were shooting their starving cattle, ending the suffering of animals so deprived of food and water that many could no longer walk. Hour after hour, the crackle of distant rifle shots penetrated the house like the dry prairie wind.

It was, Phyllis thinks, 1934. But she can't be sure of the date. It was sometime during the worst of the Great Depression and dust bowl on the flatlands of the Midwest.

The worst lasted for years.

Ice Cream and Kid Leather

Phyllis Hills Brantl was born in March 1924 on a farm near Webster, South Dakota, not far from the Minnesota border in gently rolling country known as Coteau des Prairies, "Prairie Hills." The farm was about a hundred miles northwest of Brantl's current home near Madison, Minnesota.

Brantl's father, Frank Hills, was a threshing engineer, a respected and pros-

Phyllis Hills (left) and her older sister, Byrte, about 1929. Photograph courtesy of Phyllis Hills Brantl.

perous expert in small-grain country who operated and maintained the threshing machines that harvested wheat, oats, and barley.

The 1920s, best remembered as a giddy boom time in urban and industrial America, was a modestly impoverished decade in farm country—an ominous sign of things to come. But with Frank's threshing income, the Hills family was doing well.

They had the 80-acre farm they lived on and a separate 160-acre spread a few miles north. The house was comfortably warm in winter, heated by a hard-coal stove. Frank bought a Model T Ford, one of the first private cars in the area.

Brantl can remember the day her family hosted an aunt's wedding. The house was freshly wallpapered. Embroidered curtains framed the porch windows. Five leaves broadened the dining-room table to accommodate all the breads and cakes and pies her mother was baking.

Every now and then in those days, Frank would bring home a carton of ice cream, which everyone loved. They could keep it in their icebox and savor it for days.

Brantl's older sister, Byrte, received a large and exquisite doll one Christmas. Made entirely of white kid leather, it had a china face and long curls of real hair. "I wasn't allowed to touch it," Brantl recalls.

Such memories of prosperity are faint for the aging widow. When her parents finally presented Brantl with a doll of her own, it was a small and inexpensive model from Sears. By then, everything had changed, and the cheap doll "was all they could afford and more than they should have," she says.

Snow Cream and Dust

To this day, there is no complete, definitive explanation for what caused the Great Depression of the 1930s. At the time, it was to its victims as fearsome and mysterious as a biblical plague.

Heralded by a horrifying stock market crash in October 1929, the slowdown in business activity seemed at first to be a severe but familiar cyclical economic slump. But no familiar recovery came within a year, or even two. There seemed to be no bottom.

By 1933, national income had fallen by more than half. Farm income fell 60 percent. More than one-quarter of the U.S. labor force was unemployed. Scores of thousands of businesses and banks failed. In 1933 alone, one in fifteen Minnesota farm families lost their land. At the lowest point, estimates were that thirty-four million Americans had no income whatsoever. The disaster had by then engulfed the entire industrialized world.

When it seemed the misery could get no worse, the dust bowl came to America's prairies.

Frank and Phyllis Hills in prosperous, pre-depression times, about 1929. Photograph courtesy of Phyllis Hills Brantl.

In his book *The Dirty Thirties,* Edina author William Hull shares the depression-era reminiscences of scores of Americans, including Phyllis Brantl. Hull explains that "extreme drought," the worst category known, was first reported in the Farm Belt in 1933, got worse in 1934, and struck again in 1936. Those were among the hottest and driest summers on record, and they followed harsh winters.

Dust storms roared like tidal waves of filth across the plains. Hull reports that one 1933 dust cloud covered an area stretching from Lake Superior west to Montana and south to Missouri.

Several times a week, by then, whenever a freight train would stop at the nearby rail yard, the Hills farm was visited by dirty, desperate hobos.

"Mother always fed them," Brantl recalls, often frying potatoes in pork fat. "We were a little scared of them. They were unemployed people with no place to go. They were hungry."

The aftermath of a Swift County dust storm, about 1935. Photograph courtesy of the Minnesota Historical Society.

Her family was "luckier than some," Brantl says, at least in seldom being without food, what with the farm and a garden. When the depression hit, Frank had used savings to purchase more animals—cattle, chickens, goats, pigs, sheep. There was now no threshing income to be had, so the farm had to feed the family and generate enough cash to pay the taxes. Selling cream from dairy cows was "our living," Brantl says. "Two dollars a week. We were rich."

There were other things to sell, too. Brantl's parents sold their icebox, their bathtub, their telephone, their plush front-room rug, their good dishes, their tablecloths. They sold "anything that would bring a nickel, because they had to save the farm," Brantl says.

A difference between the daughters began to grow into a barrier. "Byrte was ten years older," Brantl says. "She remembered all those things that had been sold. I hardly did."

Coal was now too expensive to use for winter fuel, so the Hillses burned straw. The big metal burner would blister the paneling while it was burning, and as soon as the straw burned out, the family shivered. They shut off most of the house and lived in two rooms.

Ice cream now was "out of the question." So in winter, the family made "snow cream." After letting it snow for a time to "clean the atmosphere," Brantl says, "you'd take a clean sheet, and let the snow pile up on it. Then, you'd take eggs and cream and vanilla and sugar and have a dish ready. You'd stir it all up and scoop in all this fresh snow and then eat it like the dickens because it was going to melt."

In summer, pounding hailstorms sometimes pummeled crops and shattered windows. Before tending to the damage, the family would make "hail cream."

"Anytime you could do something, you did it," Brantl says.

Hooverized

"Every winter morning when I get up," Brantl says now, "and step into a warm bathroom, I think, 'Oh, if only Mother could have had the heat I've got.' When I think of all Mother and Dad went through, after working so hard to have something, that's what bothers me."

Brantl's parents struggled to hold on to their farm. After five years of falling behind on tax payments, Frank had to borrow money to catch up and then had interest as well as taxes accumulating.

Brantl remembers her mother sitting up nights, worrying and sewing. She had blood pressure and heart problems, which worried Frank. As the daughters grew into teenagers, their father told them, "Bring your troubles to me. Don't worry your mother."

Elizabeth Hills, about 1938. Photograph courtesy of Phyllis Hills Brantl.

Phyllis (left), Byrte, and their cousin Charlotte were ready for a hayride with Kate in about 1929. Photograph courtesy of Phyllis Hills Brantl.

The religious family "lived around the piano," Brantl says, singing hymns and "old-time songs." At a family altar each night, her mother would read a Bible chapter. "Prayers were the only thing we had, and thank God we had those," Brantl says.

Nobody, Brantl says, knew who or what to blame for their difficulties—except for the weather and President Herbert Hoover. Hoover was widely and, many historians agree, unfairly faulted for the depression.

Brantl remembers: "If you wanted to cut something down and make it as thin and little as possible, you 'Hooverized' it. If you took too big a helping of food, somebody'd say, 'Hey, Hooverize that!'"

Byrte seemed to find others to blame, nearer to hand. It was hard for her older sister, Brantl says, to grow into a young woman with so little in the way of new and stylish clothes, especially because she remembered better times. Shoes for growing children were impossible to provide. In the spring, Phyllis and Byrte would cut the toes off the shoes they were outgrowing, the better to get through the warm months without needing a new pair.

More and more, Byrte rebelled against her parents' strict, "hard-shell Baptist" expectations—their curfews and scruples against rowdy fun.

"She was determined to go somewhere all the time, be in a crowd," Brantl says.

"I think that was her way of trying to forget, trying to crowd out her memories. She never talked about what bothered her.

"She needed people, poor girl, the way I needed animals."

They All Had Names

There were more animals than people nearby. "My father was an Englishman," Brantl says, "and the English love their animals. Byrte and I, we couldn't eat breakfast until we'd taken care of our animals. They came first. All our cows were pets. They all had names."

Brantl remembers the death of her father's beloved workhorse, Brownie, which he'd raised from a colt. A neighbor had alerted the rendering plant of the horse's death, and a truck was sent out to the farm to offer to haul away the carcass.

"My dad was a mild-mannered man," Brantl says, "but that rendering truck left in a hurry." Frank buried Brownie by himself.

Brantl's inherited devotion to animals has never diminished. Today, she runs a boarding kennel in addition to keeping about twenty dogs and cats of her own on her farm.

The suffering of cattle during the 1930s drought was pitiful, Brantl says. Besides the intense, occasional dust storms, which she describes as "blizzards of dirt," it was perpetually dry, hot, and windy.

In the pasture, the cows were "eating dirt," Brantl says. Every summer day, she

Phyllis Hills and her favorite pet cow, Sue. Photograph courtesy of Phyllis Hills Brantl.

Phyllis Brantl with Herbie in 1997. Photograph courtesy of Phyllis Hills Brantl.

and Byrte would herd their fifteen dairy cows along roadside ditches. "They'd see a patch of green, and they'd just run for it," Brantl says.

The cows would run frantically for water, too, whenever the often dry well would provide any. "They'd push each other out of the way, and you'd have to see to it that everybody got a little drink," Brantl says. The cows' eyes and nostrils were always choked with dirt.

Still, Brantl's cattle were not as malnourished and sick as most. When the federal government offered to buy farmers' cows and put them out of their misery, her pets were not included. Even so, she calls the day of the cattle shooting "the worst day I ever lived."

Workers had dug deep trenches at the dumping grounds just beyond the Hillses' property line. The bony, wretched cattle were hauled out there and led beside the trench to be shot, and then were pushed in. Some of the farmers milked their cows one last time as they waited by the trench.

To this day, Brantl says, the sound of distant gunfire during hunting season will take her back to the old farmhouse, huddled with her mother and sister, trying not to hear.

Late that afternoon, she remembers, "Dad came in. It got to him finally."

Oh, She's Fine

Both the depression and the drought eased somewhat in the late 1930s, but real economic recovery didn't occur until World War II began.

In 1943, Elizabeth Hills died of heart failure, and Frank gave up the farm he and his wife had toiled to save. He moved in with his younger daughter, who had by then begun a thirty-six-year career as a remedial reading teacher.

One Christmas soon after beginning her job, Brantl bought her father a warm winter coat. All through the depression, she says, he'd worn two thin denim jackets in the winter. "I knew he was cold. Dad was a quiet person, but I saw him smile when he opened that package."

Brantl and her father shared a home until his death in 1956. That same year, she had received a final letter from Byrte, a harsh letter venting many old resentments from the depression days.

Brantl saved Byrte's last letter for thirty years, then burned it. She has not heard word of her sister in more than forty years.

In that time, Brantl enjoyed a happy marriage and is now widowed. She has no children but many animals and memories of many kinds.

Frank had asked about Byrte in his last days. "We'd been taught never to lie, you know," Brantl says. "But I said, 'Oh, she's fine.' Sat there and lied like a trooper.

"I think about the old time more now than when I was in it," Brantl says. "I hope Mother and Dad have the nicest crowns in all heaven."

Governor Johnson and his wife, Elinor, about 1909. *St. Paul Pioneer Press* file photo

Johnson, Olson, and Stassen

Governors are not well remembered by later generations. A few Minnesota chief executives—Alexander Ramsey, John Pillsbury, Horace Austin— lent their names to places or business empires, and so achieved nominal immortality. But little is recalled about their personalities or policies.

All the same, a handful of governors transformed political life in the state, mainly by putting into words and actions the popular spirit of their times.

In the first half of the twentieth century, three great governors established the political themes that have shaped modern Minnesota. Representing the three political parties that have led the state this century, they possessed starkly differing temperaments and varied social philosophies.

Yet all three great governors, in their different ways, championed a moralistic and activist vision of government that has dominated modern Minnesota politics even more completely than it has dominated national politics. It is the belief that enlightened government can and must uphold society's standards of fairness and decency in an increasingly changeable, competitive, and impersonal modern world.

In the closing decades of the twentieth century, the evils and limits of big government became a central topic of political debate. But that only means Minnesotans ended the century quarreling over the same dispute that began it.

It's worth our while to understand the people and predicaments that got the argument of the century going.

The Progressive

John A. Johnson may have been the most personally popular governor Minnesota ever had. One of only three chief executives to carry the Democratic party label between the 1850s and the 1950s, he was elected three consecutive times by ample margins. Only a tragic, early death prevented Johnson from making an altogether serious run for the presidency.

What's more, Johnson achieved all this while overcoming the awful handicap of a disreputable profession. He was a newspaperman.

Johnson was born to Swedish immigrant parents in 1861, on a farm in the Minnesota River valley. He grew up in St. Peter, literally the son of the town drunkard, or anyhow one of the town drunkards. Impoverished by her husband's debauchery, Johnson's mother took in washing. Young John became well known around town as he picked up and dropped off customers' laundry.

By all accounts he possessed from the first the priceless political gift of effortless charm. He was tall and thin and a little frail, with a handsome and slightly melancholy face. He enjoyed life and liked people, and they liked him back.

After Johnson's death, the *Pioneer Press,* which had never supported him, admitted the journalist-turned-politician had made "political opponents but no enemies." One of Johnson's detractors once complained that the governor's main claim to greatness was that nobody could deny he was "a jolly good fellow."

But Johnson was more than that. He was a virtual archetype of the turn-of- the-century "Progressive."

No single political sentiment ever reigned so completely in America as Progressivism did in the early twentieth century. Divisions and conflicts of emphasis existed, but all parties and most politicians claimed to be "Progressive" in those days, and often supported similar policies.

Historian John Haynes has described Minnesota as late as the 1920s as being politically divided between "progressivism with a left wing" and "progressivism with a right wing."

At its core, Progressivism was a complaint about modern society—its urbanization, industrialization, materialism, and loose morals. The concentration of wealth and power in impersonal corporations and corrupt political machines was Progressivism's chief concern, but saloons, brothels, and cigarettes were also among its villains. The movement's least-attractive elements included suspicion of new immigrants and a general indifference to the plight of blacks and Indians.

In a sense, Progressivism was an optimistic revival of old-style conservatism. It was an urgent desire, especially among the politically powerful small-town middle class, to reassert society's control over unruly economic and social forces. Both modern economic liberalism and latter-day social conservatism are Progressivism's descendants.

John Johnson, Minnesota's first native-born governor and a small-town newspaper editor, was Progressivism incarnate. "No amount of schooling," he said, "can inject honor into a creature born spineless. The world wants educated men, but first it wants men of character." He decried the "selfish and high-handed course" of "intoxicated money power" and called for "heroic means to restore the country to its industrial and social equilibrium."

Johnson began political life as a Republican, a natural choice in the post–Civil War era when the GOP was nearly invincible in Minnesota. He only became a Democrat to accept the editorship of the *St. Peter Herald,* a Democratic paper in that age of an openly partisan press. It didn't take hapless Minnesota Democrats long to identify the vote-getting potential of the articulate young newspaperman.

After serving one effective term in the state senate, Johnson was nominated for governor in 1904. He won, thanks largely to bitter factional divisions in the Republican Party. Once in office, what one observer called Johnson's "easy, sprawly, comfortable" manner, along with a keen sense of public sentiment, brought him steady success.

During Johnson's three two-year terms, he promoted and oversaw the enactment of important parts of the moderate Progressive agenda. The new laws included stronger regulation of railroads, insurance companies, and industries; a constitutional amendment expanding the state's powers to tax; a new inheritance levy; and stricter protection of natural resources. Johnson also fought for workers' compensation to protect injured laborers and supported "county option" to permit alcohol prohibition at the local level. But those Progressive innovations, like others, would come later.

With considerable reluctance, Johnson, who smoked cigarettes himself, signed a bill that outlawed the new form of tobacco in Minnesota from 1909 to 1913. He also signed more liberating legislation that permitted Sunday baseball so long as the games were played "in a quiet and orderly manner."

Nothing in Johnson's program was radical. He decried what he saw as the growing concentration of power in the federal government, at the expense of states' rights, as often as he condemned "money power." He was a dead-center consensus politician with a gift for sounding like a bolder reformer than he was—a frequent formula for political success.

Johnson excelled at the grand gesture of humility. According to biographer Winifred Helmes, he once received a politically invaluable invitation to deliver the Fourth of July address at Tammany Hall in New York. The governor declined, explaining that he'd already agreed to speak at the Independence Day picnic in Luverne, Minnesota. The story made national news—more than the Tammany speech would have—and was one of many occasions when national leaders took note of this level-headed Democrat who had conquered Republican Minnesota.

Newsboys join Governor Johnson's funeral procession in a postcard image, September 1909. The postcard writer described Johnson as "the man who made St. Peter famous." *St. Paul Pioneer Press* file photo.

A national magazine profile of Johnson said: "To meet him is to like him. To talk with him is to become his friend. To know him well is to join the ranks of his admirers." Johnson won raves for a humorous speech at a Washington, D.C., dinner, in which he poked fun at uncharismatic Vice President Charles Fairbanks of Indiana, a political rival who was in the audience.

Minnesota's "production of ice," Johnson boasted to the easterners, "exceeds even that of Indiana." Even Fairbanks laughed.

Johnson was a favorite son candidate for president in 1908. But national Democrats were still enchanted with the more militant populist William Jennings Bryan. The year 1912, which became a winning one for Democrats (Woodrow Wilson was elected president), could have been Johnson's year. Eminences such as former president Grover Cleveland and steel tycoon Andrew Carnegie pronounced the Minnesotan presidential material.

"This is no ordinary man," said Carnegie. "He has future before him if he is spared."

Johnson wasn't spared. Often ill, he died from a chronic stomach ailment in 1909, at age forty-eight. As it often does, untimely death in office enlarged Johnson's virtues in the public mind. He was remembered reverently for decades as the model of a "safe and sane" reformer.

"I would have the people take back their political power," Johnson had said, "and then use it gradually, fairly, cautiously, but firmly, to save our civilization."

The Radical

Social change found a less patient Minnesota prophet in Floyd B. Olson, who led the most militant political movement ever to win significant power in America.

Olson's Farmer-Labor Party of the troubled 1930s declared capitalism "on trial for its life" and called for "the complete reorganization of the social structure," including state ownership of factories, banks, and mines.

Actual policies enacted during the Farmer-Labor era were, of course, more modest. But the movement solidified a tradition of bold Minnesota liberalism that survives to this day.

Olson was born in Minneapolis in 1891, the only child of lower-middle-class parents. He developed early a warm sympathy for the threadbare and powerless laboring classes in the city and a warm dislike for the existing economic order. He also developed a taste for what biographer George Mayer called "the conventional vices"—drinking, smoking, womanizing. Olson may have been an alcoholic.

There is no doubt he was brilliant, driven, charismatic, and lucky. He became a lawyer and landed a job with the Hennepin County Attorney's office. In 1920, the Republican county board made a colossal political blunder by appointing the bright twenty-nine-year-old Olson to serve out the term of a departing county attorney. Thus launched in politics, Olson became a scourge of Minnesota Republicans for the rest of his life.

County Attorney Olson made a name for himself by showing mercy to small-time, working-class miscreants but not to corrupt businessmen and public officials. In 1924, when he was just thirty-three, Olson won the new Farmer-Labor Party's nomination for governor. He lost and then backed away from state politics, judging that the prosperity and complacency of the 1920s made an unhealthy climate for daring political programs.

The Progressive political consensus had collapsed in the bitter loyalty crusade of World War I. Much of Progressivism's agenda had in any case been enacted, and the middle class and business community recoiled from calls for more sweeping economic change coming from struggling farmers, long organized in the Non-Partisan League, and rising labor unions.

Farmers and industrial workers had conflicting interests in many ways, but they were united in their dislike of big business. The Farmer-Labor Party was born from that common resentment. It quickly became the primary opposition to Minnesota's dominant Republicans.

When the Great Depression struck in 1929, discontent, even panic, spread like a prairie grass fire, giving Farmer-Laborites their chance to control state government. Olson was ready. Carefully softening the radical tone of party pro-

Floyd B. Olson, dashing young Hennepin County Attorney, in 1924. *St. Paul Pioneer Press* file photo.

nouncements while cultivating a broad personal political following, he won the governorship handily in 1930.

"I am not a liberal . . . I am a radical," Olson once famously declared. But his rhetoric was always more extreme and more consistent than his actions, often to the frustration of his leftist followers, some of whom considered him a mere political opportunist.

"The old pioneer idea of government confined to police power has passed off the stage," Olson said in one of his clearer summations of his philosophy. "We have now reached the socialized state. Just how far it shall extend is . . . a problem of expediency."

In three tumultuous terms as governor, Olson cajoled conservative legislatures into enacting substantial state relief for the destitute, a state income tax, a moratorium on farm foreclosures, and laws strengthening organized labor. Subtly but effectively, he sided with labor during a prolonged and violent truckers' strike in Minneapolis, helping the workers prevail in a decisive turning point for Minnesota's labor movement.

Governor Olson with presidential candidate Franklin D. Roosevelt, 1932. *St. Paul Pioneer Press* **file photo.**

Governor Olson inspects crops with Secretary of Agriculture Henry Wallace, 1933. *St. Paul Pioneer Press* file photo.

Handsome, gregarious, and a devastating debater, Olson always remained personally popular. But his political coalition eroded over time.

Olson gradually yielded to party demands for political spoils. He installed Farmer-Labor loyalists in most state jobs and required nearly all state employees to pay dues to the party. He looked the other way as outright communists infiltrated Farmer-Labor ranks, as political historian John Haynes has documented. He barely survived the 1934 election after allowing radicals to write a bluntly socialistic party platform.

Still, by 1936, Olson was running hopefully for the U.S. Senate, and many saw him as an eventual presidential contender. But that year, like Johnson before him, the downtrodden's hero died a heartbreaking early death, of cancer, at age forty-four.

The Reformer

Harold Stassen remembers being "thankful I didn't have to run against Floyd Olson."

Harold Stassen (above, center) arrives at the state capitol for his swearing in as governor, 1939, and takes the oath of office looking not a day older than his thirty-one years. *St. Paul Pioneer Press* file photos.

Stassen, second from left, as a member of a national championship rifle team, 1924. *St. Paul Pioneer Press* file photo.

But Olson, too, might have found such a contest challenging. Two years after Olson's death, Stassen single-handedly destroyed the political power of both the Farmer-Labor Party's left wing and the "standpat" conservatism of those Minnesota Republicans who resisted all labor unionism and any growth in government's role in society.

Stassen founded a brand of moderate, reformist "good government" Republicanism in Minnesota that has ever since been the main alternative to the "socialized state" vision Olson bequeathed to Minnesota liberals. Stassen Republicanism essentially accepted the socialized state and focused its efforts on arguing about "just how far it shall extend."

Stassen was born on a Dakota County farm in 1907. Idealistic and amazingly precocious, he attracted a passionate personal following at the University of Minnesota Law School. He was elected Dakota County Attorney at age twenty-three, and soon became president of the statewide county attorneys association.

In 1938, the Minnesota Young Republicans launched an improbable campaign to elect Stassen governor. Soon dubbed "the boy wonder," Stassen was thirty-one years old.

The time was right for change. Republicans were desperate for new leadership that could topple the Farmer-Labor machine. Many Minnesotans were disturbed by growing extremist influence in the Farmer-Labor Party and in some labor unions. The 1934 truckers' strike, with its bloody battles on the streets of Minneapolis, had seemed to many, Stassen recalls, "a low point of civil circumstances."

In 1937, a group of Farmer-Labor zealots temporarily occupied the state senate chamber, putting Republican lawmakers to flight. This show of disrespect for democratic institutions offended many Minnesotans.

Olson had been succeeded as governor by Farmer-Laborite Elmer Benson, a less genial and more extreme man. The story is told of a businessman remarking, after hearing Benson decry the evils of capitalism: "Floyd Olson used to *say* these things. But this sonofabitch *believes* them."

Stassen promised to reform government and labor unions, but not to turn back the clock. Backed with special passion by a rising generation of more liberal business leaders and professionals, he won in a landslide that swept Farmer-Laborites from office.

As an independent political force, the Farmer-Labor Party was finished. In the 1940s, the Democratic and Farmer-Labor parties merged to form Minnesota's Democratic-Farmer-Labor (DFL) Party. In 1948, partly in reaction to Stassen Republicanism, young anticommunist liberals led by Hubert Humphrey ousted the

Stassen as grand marshal of the Aquatennial parade in Minneapolis, 1946. *St. Paul Pioneer Press* **file photo.**

most extreme elements from the hybrid party, preparing the DFL for its powerful role in the twentieth century's second half.

Stassen admits his election in 1938 "really was quite a surprise to me, to the opposition, and to the rest of the political world." Elected three times, like Johnson and Olson, Stassen ended political spoilsmanship in Minnesota by establishing merit-based civil service; won passage of legislation to reform the finances and leadership structure of unions; helped noncommunist labor leaders oust extremists; and began a reorganization of state and local governments. Later Stassenesque Republican governors such as Luther Youngdahl and C. Elmer Anderson would improve state hospitals, expand educational funding, and destroy an illegal gambling industry.

Stassen's "new day" Republicanism looked like nothing so much as an updated rebirth of Progressivism—earnest, moralistic, practical. But Stassen's passion was for international affairs. As governor, he became an early advocate for American intervention to defeat Nazi Germany, a controversial position at the time. He practiced what he preached, resigning the governorship in 1943 to join the U.S. Navy.

Visionary and intellectually gifted, Stassen lacked the personal magnetism of Olson and Johnson. Journalist William White credited Stassen with "the most profound absence of a sense of humor in American politics." His somewhat remote personality, combined with bad luck, prevented Stassen from achieving his abiding ambition to become president.

After serving as a delegate to the United Nations Charter Conference in 1945, Stassen was a serious candidate for president in 1948, narrowly losing the nomination to Thomas Dewey of New York. Then the ascendancy of World War II giant Dwight Eisenhower blocked Stassen's best opportunities to make another credible run for the White House.

Stassen became a cabinet-level adviser to Eisenhower on arms control and foreign affairs, always favoring negotiations with the Soviet Union, whose eventual collapse he predicted as early as 1951.

From 1960 on, Stassen conducted a long series of increasingly unlikely campaigns for president. It is as an aging, perennial dreamer that many Minnesotans remember Stassen today.

If that is an ironic fate for Minnesota's "boy wonder," it is also an underestimation of a politician who, like the other great governors, deftly responded to the circumstances of his time and left an indelible mark on his state.

Television cameramen have the candidate all to themselves as Stassen announces his tenth campaign for the presidency in 1991. Photograph by Scott Takushi; *St. Paul Pioneer Press* file photo.

Loyalist troops assault a rebel position during the Spanish civil war. In three years of brutal fighting, a military uprising overthrew an elected government and served as a dress rehearsal for World War II. Several thousand foreign idealists, including a few Minnesotans such as Clarence Forester, fought for the ill-fated Spanish Republic. Photograph from AP/Wide World Photos; reprinted with permission.

A HAVE-NOT'S WAR

The Spanish Civil War, 1937–38

Ernest Hemingway's *For Whom the Bell Tolls* is the most famous of many books written about the Spanish civil war of the 1930s.

The novelist described the feeling shared by American volunteers in that faraway and long-ago struggle as "a feeling of consecration to a duty toward all the oppressed of the world," an almost "religious experience" of "absolute brotherhood." And "the best thing was that there was something you could do about this feeling. . . . You could fight."

Clarence Forester of north Minneapolis was one of the Americans who had that feeling. During a violent truck drivers' strike in Minneapolis in 1934, he had learned, he says, "that sometimes to get the rights you should have, they're not just given to you, you have to fight for them."

In November 1996, Forester celebrated his eighty-first birthday in Spain. But he felt, he says, "like I was twenty-three again." In 1937 and 1938, Forester had passed his twenty-second and twenty-third birthdays in the warm and fervent land of bullfights and flamenco dances.

Forester went back as one of 380 aging veterans who served in the Spanish civil war as part of "international brigades." They were guests of the Spanish government for an emotional weeklong tribute to their unsuccessful struggle six decades earlier to defend the Spanish Republic against a military uprising.

The old soldiers returned, many aboard wheelchairs or armed with canes, to be cheered and hugged by crowds of Spaniards who mostly knew of the veterans' deeds only through history books and stories told.

Nobody has ever outcheered or outhugged the Spanish. Mingling with impassioned 1996 crowds, Forester thought back to the throngs that had saluted the international brigades as they left Spain in November 1938 at a moment when the war was going badly for the Republic and final defeat was near.

"Somewhere," Forester says he kept thinking, "I'm going to get hugged by somebody who hugged me in 1938." Small children of the war years, he figures, would have been in their mid-sixties by the time he returned.

Forester has lived most of his life between his two pilgrimages to Spain: fighting for America in World War II, working a career as a machinist, and enjoying a happy forty-seven-year marriage.

But the impetuous, idealistic crusade in Spain, Forester agrees, has remained the defining event of his life.

Radicalized

Forester had always been what he calls a "have-not." He was born in 1915 in the little town of Alfred, North Dakota, the ninth of ten children. The family was poor and got poorer when Forester's father died. At fifteen, having had scarcely any schooling, Forester snuck aboard a freight train and headed for Minneapolis.

Soon he moved to Superior, Wisconsin, where he lived for several years with two older half-brothers. They were "well-established radicals," Forester says, "and I did a lot of reading there."

By the time he returned to Minneapolis, Forester was "radicalized," he says. "I would have to say that I was an extreme leftist," he adds.

He also recalls that a person could get labeled a "commie bastard" during the 1930s for advocating such programs as Social Security and unemployment insurance, which are now "sacred cows to everybody."

The early 1930s were bleak depression years. Forester was then part of a ragtag army of unemployed men, frightened and angry, often homeless, often hungry. He frequented the Gateway skid-row district of downtown Minneapolis.

At the Gateway, Forester says, "You could always find a rabble-rouser making a spiel: socialists, communists, unionists. And the Salvation Army. The Army had a band there, and there would be some preaching. And then you could follow the band to their headquarters and get a half sandwich and a bowl of soup."

The world was ablaze with political passions. Everywhere, economic desperation fanned the flames of bitter class and ethnic conflicts. Utopian dreams billowed from a bonfire of harsh realities.

In America, pressure for expanded rights and political power for workers and the poor led to sometimes violent battles over unionization and to the controversial, government-enlarging New Deal programs of Franklin Roosevelt. In Minnesota, the left-leaning Farmer-Labor Party was in power through much of the decade.

Overseas, ideological blazes burned out of control. In the Soviet Union, a brutal communist regime claimed to be the spearhead of a worldwide struggle for

Clarence Forester holds his honorary Spanish citizenship documents outside his north Minneapolis home in 1997. Photograph by Janet Hostetter for the *St. Paul Pioneer Press.*

equality and workers' rights. In Germany, Italy, and Japan, fascist dictatorships, militaristic and racist, claimed to be defending national purity against modern decadence and left-wing revolution.

A cataclysm was coming. In 1936, crusaders and aggressors from around the world descended on Spain for a deadly free-for-all that became the dress rehearsal for World War II.

Forester was at center stage.

The Thing to Do

Spain had suffered political turmoil since the latter nineteenth century. Ethnic separatist movements worsened conflicts between a desperately poor peasantry and a rigid, old-world ruling class. In 1931, a broad-based uprising overthrew Spain's king and established a republic. For several years, an elected government of moderate socialists presided over Spain's most optimistic days.

But extremists of both the right and the left were not content. Violent strikes, assassinations, and revelations of corruption destabilized the republic and weakened centrist political leaders.

In early 1936, a more militant left-wing government was elected. That summer, the Spanish army rose in revolt, led by General Francisco Franco, a violent and inflexible nationalist who would become Spain's answer to Germany's Hitler and Italy's Mussolini.

Hitler and Mussolini themselves were eager to test their war machines and to set up a sympathetic regime in Spain. They quickly sent Franco massive support, including aircraft, artillery, tanks, and some fifty thousand troops. Soviet dictator Joseph Stalin sent less generous help to the Republican side, while encouraging hard-line Spanish leftists to fight for control of the besieged government.

The various dictators' interventions prevented either side from winning a quick victory. The Spanish civil war slowed to a vicious grind.

Far away in Minneapolis, Clarence Forester was following events in Spain and growing indignant over the nonintervention policy and arms embargo the United States had implemented, along with most other democracies.

On January 21, 1937, a delegation of Spanish college students touring the United States appeared at a rally at the old Minneapolis Auditorium. Thousands listened to the students plead for American assistance to the Spanish Republic. Forester was there. He had heard volunteer soldiers were also being sought. That night, he says, "I made up my mind that going to Spain was the thing to do."

The war's end brings a reunion for two brothers who fought on opposite sides. The brother in the helmet served in Francisco Franco's rebel army, while the brother in the beret fought for the Republic. Photograph from AP/Wide World Photos; reprinted with permission.

It may seem a peculiar decision all these decades later. But the Spanish civil war was an international sensation in the embattled 1930s. The cause of the Spanish Republic was utterly enthralling to left-leaning people of that time. To them, it seemed to flawlessly embody an eternal struggle of all that was idealistic and forward-looking against all that was petrified and hateful.

Nearly forty thousand *brigadistas* from forty countries, including twenty-seven hundred Americans, made the same decision Forester did.

"It just seemed to me," Forester remembers, "that if something wasn't done, Hitler would take over everything. The Japanese were on the march. It looked like sooner or later we were going to have trouble. Spain was the first opportunity to do something about it. For me, it wasn't that different from going on that [truck drivers'] picket line in 1934."

Forester enlisted in what became known as the Abraham Lincoln Brigade. It was illegal to travel to Spain, but a recruiter gave Forester a bus ticket to New York City. In Manhattan, he was to "stand on a particular street corner and hold my suitcase in my left hand." Someone came along and put him on a ship for France. Stage by stage in the same surreptitious manner—by train, taxi, and on foot—he was guided through France and across the Pyrenees into Spain.

"At the time," Forester says, "I didn't know who was organizing [the volunteer effort]. But it was the Communist International. The money probably came from Moscow."

On the ship going over, Forester ate all he wanted for the first time in his life.

When a Lot of the Lincolns Got Killed

Forester served with Republican artillery units from March 1937 until November 1938. He tells no detailed combat stories, but says he was there "when a lot of the Lincolns got killed" during a disastrous retreat across the Ebro River.

Casualties were shocking throughout the Spanish civil war. About nine hundred Americans were killed, a full third of those who served. Altogether, counting Franco's postwar purges, the conflict took more than five hundred thousand lives.

Forester remembers meeting Hemingway on the Fourth of July in 1937, when a group of American writers visited the Lincoln Brigade at the front. Already famous for his tragic stories of stoic heroes, the eventual Nobel Prize winner distributed beer and cigars. He invited the troops to come up to his Madrid hotel room for a shower should they ever get the chance. (Forester didn't.)

Forester thought the swaggering Hemingway "was a pretty nice guy. A lot of people thought he was a booze hound and a womanizer. Well, if that was his life, it shouldn't bother me."

The fate of Hemingway's book illustrated Americans' conflicting feelings about the Spanish civil war. A runaway best-seller, *For Whom the Bell Tolls* was unanimously voted the Pulitzer Prize for 1940. But the award was never given because of the political sensitivity of Hemingway's sympathies for the Spanish left.

Yet, the left was also disappointed. Hemingway's book portrayed infighting and incompetence within Republican forces. It also described atrocities committed by the left behind the lines. (These never involved American volunteers and were matched by Franco's side.)

Franco, at all events, won the war, taking Madrid in March 1939. Five months earlier, the Republic had sent Forester and all the other foreign volunteers home, in a final, futile attempt to win decisive international sympathy.

Impressed with Them People

Within five years, Forester was back in war-torn Europe, fighting in the U.S. Army throughout the 1944–45 drive across France and Germany. He was there at the liberation of the Buchenwald concentration camp—a sight, he says, that "really proved to me I did the right thing in going to Spain."

Among the Buchenwald inmates, Forester found about thirty Spaniards who had fled into France at the end of the civil war. It gave him pleasure to scrounge extra cigarettes, candy bars, and rations for them.

"I was impressed with them people," he says of the Spanish. "They were the first ones who put up any meaningful resistance to fascism."

Forester says other GIs observing the horrors of Buchenwald gained an understanding of why Americans like him had volunteered to fight fascism in Spain. Yet, America as a whole has never been sure what to think of the Lincoln Brigade.

Lincoln Brigade veterans often suffered discrimination as suspected communists, particularly during the 1950s cold war "McCarthy era." Forester himself lost a job with a military contractor because of his service in Spain. The organization of Lincoln Brigade veterans was for many years accused of being a communist front organization.

Today, Forester says, many Spaniards seem to think "it's time to forget" the hatreds of the civil war, although that is difficult. For his part, Forester remains bitter that America "is the only country where the government has never in some way indicated that to have fought fascism in Spain was the honorable thing to do." He angrily decries the support the American government gave to Franco's regime over many years.

Franco kept Spain out of World War II. He governed harshly until his death in 1975, when power was transferred to Franco's handpicked successor, King Juan

Carlos, heir to the ancient Spanish throne. The king quickly restored democracy to Spain. He serves to this day as a constitutional monarch.

In 1996, a freely elected conservative government took power in Spain. Conservative leaders did not cancel that year's tributes to the *brigadistas,* planned by earlier socialist governments. The conservative leadership, however, did not attend. For the old veterans, Forester says, their heroes' welcome in Spain was "the most wonderful experience of our lives."

"I know from personal experience," Forester says, "what it's like to be hungry and homeless." After the war, he says, he found a trade as a machinist and "learned what it's like to have a good life," complete with a house and a Cadillac. His wife, Hazel, whom he'd married in 1941, died in 1987. They had no children.

"What's always still with me is the difference between the haves and the have-nots," Forester says. "I'll never get rid of that. I'm glad to have been a have-not. And I can feel I almost became a have. Almost is close enough for me."

Mending nets was a constant chore for the fishermen and their families. Young Stuart Sivertson assists Stanley Sivertson with net work on their cabin's front porch. Photograph courtesy of Howard Sivertson.

Isle Royale Fishing

Howard Sivertson's open boat was twenty-four feet long. He remembers that as he climbed one wind-driven wave after another, crouching in the stern clinging desperately to the tiller, he would watch the boat's bow rise nearly to vertical above him.

Even then, each advancing wall of frigid, black water loomed several feet above the bow, where it curled over on itself and came crashing down on the twelve-year-old fisherman.

Lake Superior, the temperamental giant of the Great Lakes and one of the most dangerous waters on Earth, has swallowed far sturdier vessels and far more seasoned mariners. With the special vividness that brushes with death bestow, and with more than a touch of pride, Sivertson recalls the day a sudden August squall on Superior nearly ended his young life.

Today, Sivertson clings tenaciously to all memories of his boyhood. He is among the last survivors of a lost culture—a society of immigrant fishing families that for more than a century toiled and thrived on Minnesota's freshwater sea, braving Superior's many moods with traditional techniques and precious little technology.

A painter and an author, Sivertson has become the chronicler of an adventurous way of life that has all but vanished before his eyes.

"There's a loneliness," Sivertson says, "in knowing you're the last of something."

Huck Finn Paradise

There had not been even a hint of dawn that August morning when Sivertson heard his parents stirring.

As always, his mother, Myrtle, had risen first, at about four o'clock, to light the wood-burning stove and get breakfast started. Not long after, the boy and his

Howard Sivertson near his
home in Grand Marais in
1998. Photograph by Josh
Meltzer of the *Duluth News-
Tribune.*

father, Art, trudged down to the dock below the house—damp and cold in early
morning, even in August—to load nets and buoys into their wide wooden boat.

Sivertson began his workdays by siphoning fuel into the tank of the "gas boat"
(so-called to distinguish it from a "sail boat"). He remembers breakfasts of oatmeal
slightly flavored with gasoline. Typically, work would end some seventeen hours
later, after the day's catch of several hundred pounds of lake trout had been cleaned
and packed in ice and all the equipment was prepared for the next day's fishing.
They worked like that seven days a week.

The Sivertsons were one of about a hundred families who, when Howard was
a boy, spent the April-to-November fishing season on Isle Royale. The "Isle" is
actually a dense, fifty-three-mile-long archipelago of rocky islands, twelve miles
out into Superior's misty deeps off the Minnesota-Ontario coast. It had been a
favorite fishing spot for Indian harvesters going back thousands of years.

Beginning in the mid-nineteenth century, Scandinavian immigrants found their
way to Isle Royale and Minnesota's North Shore, along which another four hundred families fished in the early decades of this century. All across the Midwest,
Norwegian and Swedish settlers were creating a lively consumer market for fish.
For those, like Sivertson's forebears, with a seafaring background amid Norway's
fjords, the wave-battered Superior coastlines, jagged with forbidding cliffs and
treacherous reefs, felt like home.

When Sivertson was born in 1930, the North Shore highway had existed barely
five years. People remembered the days when such hearty men as John Beargrease,

for whom a famed Duluth-to-Grand Portage dogsled race is named, had provided the main contact with civilization through much of the year, delivering mail and supplies up and down the shore by dogsled or rowboat. Sivertson says the half century of daring and stamina displayed by such northwoods adventurers put the West's more famous Pony Express to shame.

Out on Isle Royale, what Sivertson calls the "pioneer life" continued through his boyhood in the 1930s and 1940s. There was no electricity, no running water, no movie theater, no roads. Large steamships operated by wholesale fish companies in Duluth triggered festive occasions when they called twice a week to pick up the fishermen's heavy boxes of iced lake trout or salted herring and to drop off deliveries. Otherwise, the island community was on its own.

It was a "Huck Finn paradise" for young children, Sivertson says, where moose were so common they were considered pests and the opportunities for hunting, fishing, and exploring were inexhaustible. "Island brats" fearlessly swam in Superior's bracing waters and "survived hypothermia every day of our lives," Sivertson says.

Sivertson treasured the island's close-knit, interdependent community. His grandparents and various uncles, aunts, and cousins all lived nearby. "Almost every-

The Sivertsons, about 1935 (left to right): Howard, Art, Myrtle, and Betty. Photograph courtesy of Howard Sivertson.

Howard Sivertson's grand-
parents, Theodora and Sam,
who arrived on Isle Royale in
1892. Photograph courtesy
of Howard Sivertson.

body was a relative," he says, "and everybody was a friend, even though they were
competitors, too. People depended on each other. They were entertainment for
each other. . . . We felt loved."

Sivertson's grandparents, who had arrived on the island in 1892, had a home
on Washington Harbor at Isle Royale's western tip, enjoying a fine sunset view.

"On especially nice evenings," Sivertson says, "people would wander down
there, or row down in their boats, until there were fifteen or twenty adults standing on the porch. Then somebody would break out the concertina, and they'd sing
old country songs." The favorites were sentimental ballads about immigrants long-
ing for loved ones left behind across the sea.

The toil was exhausting and relentless for commercial fishing families, the
profits modest and uncertain. Many women, including Sivertson's mother, found
island life grueling—hauling all their water in buckets from the lake, cooking and
cleaning and mending not only for their own families, but also for the bachelor
fishermen their husbands hired as helpers.

Boat Day was a festive occasion on Isle Royale in the heyday of the fishing culture. Twice each week, steamers would stop to deliver supplies and mail and pick up fish. In the photographs, the steamer *America* draws a crowd in the 1920s; and Myrtle and Betty Sivertson enjoy Boat Day in about 1930, with the steamer *Winyah* in the background. Photographs courtesy of Howard Sivertson.

Sivertson recalls the familiar sight of his mother, sound asleep over her dishpan after dinner, her weary features lit by the glow of a kerosene lamp.

Integration

The rising sun was in Sivertson's face as he and his father motored toward their fishing grounds that August morning. Already it was becoming a fine, warm day, the vast lake as still as a puddle.

The Sivertsons' fishing grounds were off McCormick Reef on the southwest end of Isle Royale. By custom, each fisherman claimed his fishing grounds by being the first to fish a given spot in the spring. Thereafter, all the other fishermen respected his possession of those grounds for that season.

Sivertson and his father set their three-hundred-foot-long nets in shallow water near the reef. The best fishing of the year began in August, as lake trout moved into the shallows to spawn. Deep hook-line fishing in the spring was harder and less productive. In October, fishing stopped for three weeks to allow the fish to spawn and renew their population. About once a season, dozens of community members would cooperate to net and process large schools of herring that would appear in island bays.

It was common for a twelve-year-old son to begin his own fishing career as an apprentice to his father. Yet, it was clear from early on, Sivertson says, that he was not destined to continue the family tradition.

Prone to seasickness, Sivertson was also, by his own account, too dreamy, inattentive, and awkward to be a good fisherman. This was a frustration to his father,

Howard, his mother, Myrtle, and sister, Betty, aboard a small boat with Isle Royale behind them, about 1940. Photograph courtesy of Howard Sivertson.

Isle Royale fishermen set
their nets in a slight swell
on Washington Harbor.
Photograph courtesy of
Howard Sivertson.

who "moved around that boat like a cat." Unlike most Isle Royale fishermen, Sivertson's father generally preferred to fish alone. "And after I started fishing with him," Sivertson says, "he preferred it even more."

Still, Sivertson prized the traditional folk culture's integration of work with family, home, and community. Laboring close to nature, the fishing families understood the meaning of their work, Sivertson says, and had little need to seek "escape" in "recreation." They respected nature and protected the environment because their lives depended on it.

"We caught the fish, cleaned the fish, shipped the fish, ate the fish," Sivertson says.

Sivertson and his father were shirtless and relaxed, basking in a rare balmy day on Superior, when they "started to see a roll. The seas started getting big, and all of a sudden, Dad said, 'We gotta get out of here.' The storm hit so fast we just barely could get the boat turned around toward home."

It was the kind of freak Superior storm that often ruined fishermen financially, destroying nets and other gear that couldn't be retrieved, and occasionally killed them. The worst storms—blizzards on the lake—hit in the autumn. Lost fishermen were sometimes found in their boats, frozen to their oars, solid as sculptures.

"Pounding" into the furious wind, the Sivertsons spotted one of their hired men, his boat tangled in netting and threatening to capsize. Sivertson's father jumped into the hired man's boat to help, calling back to his son, "Stay in deep water, outside the reefs!"

But the frightened boy's instinct was to stay close to shore. Soon, he was caught inside the reefs, where the seas piled up to monstrous heights.

"I was a little scared," Sivertson says, with admirable Norwegian understatement.

Invaders

It didn't require a gloomy Scandinavian outlook to see that, by the 1940s, Superior's commercial fishing culture was doomed. Some biologists believe the commercial fishing pressure was, in the long run, unsustainable for cold, infertile Superior.

A more imminent threat was smelt. Introduced into the lake in the hope they would become valuable forage for other fish species, smelt instead became predators of lake trout eggs and fry. By the late 1940s, the opening of the Saint Lawrence Seaway helped bring in the lamprey eel, which further decimated the trout population.

Another invader was even more powerful. In 1931, a year after Sivertson's birth, Congress passed a law turning Isle Royale into a national park. The drive was on to preserve recreational opportunities for Americans, particularly in "wilderness" settings.

National Park Service officials made their position clear. The fishing families were "not conducive to the wilderness aspect of Isle Royale," Sivertson recalls them repeating. "Here were hardworking fishermen," he adds, "who'd been kind to the environment, kept it in good enough shape that the government wanted to make a park out of it. Now they had to leave."

Gradually imposing ever more restrictions on the fishing families' use of Isle Royale's resources, the government established a rule under which families who did not own their island property (the large majority) could continue to fish only so long as they returned every season. If they missed a year, their houses would be bulldozed and burned. The Sivertsons' place was torched in 1957.

Sivertson doesn't conceal his resentment for the recreational ethic that destroyed the culture he loved. "We had slow, wooden boats, kerosene lamps, outhouses. The Park Service came in with fast fiberglass boats and modern houses, blasting holes to create septic systems and running water. . . . It wasn't until the government got out there to create a pristine wilderness that you got the first electric generators on the island," he says.

Today, many thousands of visitors each year use Isle Royale's hiking trails, lodging, and camping facilities. Sport anglers control the fishery, which has come back to health as the smelt and lamprey have been controlled.

"A whole culture had to leave Isle Royale so they could create a wilderness," Sivertson says. Instead, he complains, "they've made a recreational park out of it."

Art Sivertson feeds gulls following his fishing boat, about 1940. Photograph courtesy of Howard Sivertson.

Today, barely a dozen commercial fishermen remain on the North Shore. On Isle Royale, Sivertson's uncle, Stan, was the last commercial fisherman. He died in 1994.

Picturing the Past

After many frigid and frightening hours, the twelve-year-old Sivertson made it safely home through the August storm.

"Kinda rough, huh?" was his father's entire tribute to the boy's accomplishment. Sivertson's interest in a fishing career was not increased by the experience.

Following a twenty-five-year stint as a commercial artist, Sivertson moved to a backwoods cabin in 1976 and started painting for himself. He was back to using an outhouse, realizing that "if I wanted to go to the bathroom in the house, I couldn't afford to do what I wanted."

Describing himself as a "narrative painter," Sivertson has spent the past two decades rendering the landscapes and history of the North Shore and Lake Superior. He has published three books of paintings and accompanying stories, including *Once upon an Isle,* a lovingly detailed tribute to the community he once knew.

He still visits Isle Royale often. In 1990 and 1991, Sivertson worked on the island as a "cultural demonstrator," operating a replica of a commercial fishery the Park Service now includes among the park's attractions, having been persuaded that the human heritage of Isle Royale is a proper part of its story.

Sivertson lives today in Grand Marais with his second wife, Elaine, also an artist. He sells his paintings through three galleries operated by artist daughters— in Grand Marais, Duluth, and Bayfield, Wisconsin.

There is irony, and perhaps justice, in the fact that many of Sivertson's works are today purchased by tourists who share the painter's admiration for a way of life the culture of recreation has displaced.

Officers of the 109th Engineer Battalion, early 1943, preparing to go into battle in Tunisia against the German Africa Corps. Left to right: Lieutenant Ted Karge would be severely wounded; Lieutenant Scott Creighton (with kitten) would be killed; Lieutenant Royal Lee would be taken prisoner and spend the rest of the war in POW camps; Lieutenant Joe Baker and Captain John Webb would survive the war unharmed. Photograph courtesy of Royal Lee.

The POWs' Secret War, 1943–45

The old German army truck bounced down a cobblestone road in northwestern Poland. Lieutenant Royal Lee and two other U.S. Army officers bounced along in the back of the truck, guarded by two German soldiers.

The guards were in an easygoing mood. They were happy to have an afternoon's duty away from the nearby prisoner-of-war camp. Lee and the other two POWs would be doing all the work.

Lee tried to look relaxed, too. POWs would naturally have been pleased to be spending a day outside their cramped, barbed-wire world. The day's errand was a happy one of picking up a shipment of packages for the camp—packages from home.

But Lee wasn't feeling relaxed. He was "concerned"—an emotion he says he felt frequently during his two years in Nazi POW camps. "You were concerned," he says, "because you didn't know what would happen if you got caught doing what you were doing."

It was June 1944, the month the D-Day invasion of France began the decisive Allied assault against Nazi Germany. A thousand miles behind the battle lines, Lee and his fellow POWs also continued waging the war, fighting as best they could along what was called the "barbed-wire front."

The humanitarian packages that Lee and the others were to pick up that afternoon would include two fraudulent parcels sent by the U.S. War Department. These would contain not sardines, cigarettes, and coffee, as most packages did, but two .22-caliber automatic pistols. Lee's job was to help sneak the guns past the Nazis.

Lee was part of an elaborate, top-secret network that kept American and British POWs well supplied with contraband and constantly attempting escapes throughout World War II. Only in the 1990s was the story of this "escape factory" made public, allowing veterans of the effort to share their long-untold stories.

A boyish Lee in dress uniform, 1941. Photograph courtesy of Royal Lee.

Lee, a retired insurance man in Mankato, says that when he describes his adventures in Nazi POW camps, people sometimes think he's "seen one too many episodes of *Hogan's Heroes.*"

The Whole Damn Army

Lee was born in 1916 in Madison, South Dakota, the only child of middle-class parents. He attended the University of South Dakota and graduated in 1939, the year World War II broke out in Europe.

Lee immediately joined the military, commissioned as a second lieutenant because of his education. In the winter of 1942–43, in North Africa, he was among the first American troops to take on the Nazi war machine.

In those early battles, the Americans were outgunned and outmaneuvered. Lee was in command of a fifty-man infantry platoon in February 1943, when a German attack overran American forces in Tunisia. Lee and his men were trapped forty miles behind the German lines. Taken prisoner, they were marched to a temporary POW enclosure, where they joined thousands of other captured Americans.

"It looked like they had the whole damn army," Lee remembers.

Life as a POW began with interrogation. Lee refused to tell his Nazi questioners anything beyond his name, rank, and serial number, as required by the Geneva Convention.

Lee shaving in the field during training maneuvers, 1941. Photograph courtesy of Royal Lee.

In training camp, Lee enjoys an elegant dinner with guests. Photograph courtesy of Royal Lee.

Later, he says, "One of the boys in my platoon came over and said, 'Lieutenant, I'm going to be your orderly. The Germans asked me if I knew any of the officers out here and what unit they were from. They said if I could identify them, I could go along with them as their orderly.'

"It was just a ruse," Lee says, to discover where various units had been deployed, a valuable bit of military information. "He didn't go with me as my orderly."

Officers and enlisted men were soon separated. On a cargo plane carrying some forty captured officers to Italy, Lee got his first glimpse of the ceaseless battle of wits that would be waged between POWs and their captors.

There was only one guard on the plane, and the prisoners quickly hatched a scheme to overpower the guard and the pilots and fly the plane to freedom.

But the Germans knew what they were doing. The plane crossed the Mediterranean at a frighteningly low altitude, just a few feet above the waves. The hazardous altitude made any attempt to attack the pilots suicidal.

In May 1943, having crossed Europe by boxcar, Lee arrived at Oflag 64, a prison camp for American officers near the town of Schubin in Poland. There, he was soon drawn into an intercontinental escape conspiracy.

Super-dupers

When the old army truck pulled up to the railroad depot in Schubin, Lee and the two other POWs got busy unloading humanitarian parcels from a freight car. Their guards found a shady spot to lounge and enjoy the cigarettes the Americans had given them.

The POWs made a list of prisoners receiving packages. But they were careful to make no record of two packages addressed to POWs named Grimm and Howard.

There were no POWs by those names at Oflag 64. These were the phony parcels containing guns, sent by a mysterious military-intelligence service agency called MIS-X.

The full story of MIS-X was first told in a 1990 book, *The Escape Factory,* by Lloyd Shoemaker, who worked for the agency. Publication of the book has freed veterans, such as Lee, to talk about experiences they had kept to themselves for half a century. Sworn to secrecy when he was discharged from military service, Lee had never even told his wife, Harriet, whom he'd married in 1945.

The idea behind the secrecy was that MIS-X tricks might come in handy in some future war, if the techniques remained unknown.

MIS-X was established soon after America entered the war in 1941. It was modeled after a British operation. The purpose was to stay in contact with POWs throughout Europe by means of coded letters, and to help them attempt escapes, largely by smuggling "escape aids" into the camps.

MIS-X operated a literal "escape factory" in suburban Washington, D.C. Technicians there concealed contraband in innocuous items that could be sent to POWs under the names of bogus humanitarian organizations.

Maps of the regions surrounding POW camps were inserted between the cardboard layers of chessboards, or glued in fragments to the backs of playing cards. Baseballs were wound around radio components. Tiny saw blades and compasses were hidden in shaving brushes or cribbage boards. Money, cameras, travel documents, clothing, flashlights, and much more were successfully slipped into POW camps by MIS-X.

Not to mention pistols.

The packages addressed to fictional POWs Grimm and Howard were what MIS-X called "super-dupers," according to Shoemaker. These were used when the contraband that POWs needed could not be effectively camouflaged. Super-duper packages were addressed to nonexistent POWs, and it was left to the prisoners themselves to somehow sneak the "hot" parcels past their Nazi captors.

Tame Guards

Heavy with POW parcels, the old army truck entered Oflag 64 late in the afternoon. It passed through the single gate in a double barbed-wire fence that stood eight feet tall and stretched about three hundred yards long on each side of the camp.

The prison compound surrounded a former boarding school for girls. One of the old brick dormitories housed the "tin stores" where POW packages were received and inspected.

"Tin" is a British term for a tin can. At the tin stores, German censors would inspect every package arriving for POWs, and would puncture every can containing food. This prevented POWs from building up a supply of food to use in escapes.

"Super-duper" packages had to be slipped past the Germans uninspected. Lee and the other tin stores workers would stand at one end of a long table, opening parcels and pushing them down the table toward the Nazi censor.

Then, Lee remembers, "You'd start stacking the parcels up. You'd get so many stacked up they couldn't keep track of them.

"Then, you'd offer the guard a cigarette. Somebody would suggest brewing a pot of coffee. You'd distract them, and then somebody would pick up the hot package and quick move it over to the pile of packages by the door that had already been checked."

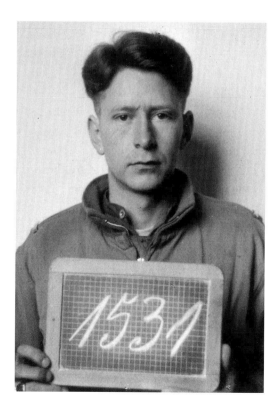

Royal Lee's POW identification photo. Photograph courtesy of Royal Lee.

In this way, the automatic pistols sent by MIS-X entered Oflag 64 unmolested. To Lee's knowledge, no contraband was ever intercepted at that camp.

Many guards at Oflag 64, as at many compounds housing American and British POWs, were older soldiers. Often less than fanatical Nazis, many were also less than perfectly hostile to Americans.

"You'd be surprised," Lee recalls, "how often they'd say, 'Hey, I've got a cousin in Milwaukee,' or 'I've got a sister in Nebraska.'"

The success of MIS-X in Europe owed much to the comparatively humane treatment Germans often extended to American and British POWs—at least in allowing humanitarian parcels to reach prisoners. In the Pacific war, the Japanese were much harsher to POWs, as Japanese military culture considered surrender dishonorable. MIS-X accomplished little in the Pacific theater, according to Shoemaker.

Meanwhile, Russian POWs, Polish civilians, and, of course, Jews and many others were brutally abused by Nazis, as Lee sometimes witnessed. On occasion, he says, Oflag 64 would be visited by "mean suckers" from the Gestapo or the SS.

But Oflag 64 inmates often succeeded famously in fooling and manipulating their everyday guards.

"Most everybody is subject to a little blackmail," Lee says. Guards were bribed with cigarettes, coffee, candy bars, and other wartime luxuries that POWs possessed. (MIS-X made sure they always had plenty.) Oflag 64 POWs built a radio, called a "bird," with parts obtained through such bribes, Lee says.

When the bribed guard became fearful and refused to bring any more "bird" materials, Lee says he was told: "By God, you better bring what we need, or they're going to find out where we got the rest of this stuff."

Once maneuvered into such a helpless position, a guard was called "tame."

Escape efforts, Lee says, were constantly in motion. A group of five senior officers approved or disapproved all escape schemes. Tailors fabricated civilian clothes and German army uniforms for escapees. Documents were forged. Keys were fashioned from pieces of tin cans.

To safeguard such doings, an elaborate deployment of "stooges" was maintained. POWs would station themselves at key points throughout the camp, each stooge within sight of one other. Approaching guards or other dangers would be indicated by prearranged signals—closing an open book, shifting from a sitting to a standing position. The warning would be instantly relayed by all the stooges across the compound.

Often, POWs harassed their captors mischievously. They would throw cans or other debris into the barbed-wire fences to set off alarms and "irritate them a bit" (as well as to monitor how the guards responded). During roll calls, especially in darkness, POWs would change positions in line to confuse the guards' count. They would plant cigarettes or other items on guards they disliked; then, they'd complain of those very items being stolen and demand that camp personnel be searched.

Escapes seldom succeeded. Shoemaker reports that of some 96,000 American POWs in Europe, 737 made "home runs"—escaping captivity and returning safely to their commands.

But the antics of MIS-X and the POWs had a serious military purpose—to enlist prisoners as still-active combatants, causing the Nazis as many headaches and distractions as possible.

Eventually, the strategy became so successful that the Nazis struck back.

Great Escapes

The most ambitious escape attempts usually involved tunneling. At Oflag 64, Lee says, a 150-foot tunnel was dug that began beneath a barracks stove, stretching out beyond the camp fence and into a nearby wood.

Not the least of the many challenges in such an uncanny project was disposing of the dirt excavated from the tunnel. POWs used what they indelicately called "peckers"—long cloth tubes that could be filled with dirt and concealed in one's pant leg. Pulling on a string would open the tube's bottom and release the dirt onto the camp grounds, where many tons of soil were thus concealed.

Though it was never discovered by the Germans, Oflag 64's tunnel was never used. In spring 1944, senior officers canceled plans for a mass escape, citing the atrocious consequences of what became known as "the Great Escape," an event immortalized in books and movies.

On March 24, 1944, seventy-six British air officers escaped from Stalag Luft III in eastern Germany through a 335-foot tunnel. All but three of the escapees were soon captured, but the venture had been only too successful in traumatizing the Nazis.

Adolf Hitler was so enraged by the mounting audacity of POWs that he ordered the Gestapo to shoot fifty of the recaptured British officers. This was done. Soon thereafter, notices went up at all POW camps, including Oflag 64, announcing that escape would no longer be considered "a sport."

Yet within months, an even more ambitious escape was plotted at Oflag 64. The new scheme called for a coordinated POW uprising and commando assault that would rescue the entire camp and carry four hundred POWs to freedom aboard B-17 aircraft that would land in nearby fields. It was for this operation that the automatic pistols were requested and sent.

But in the end, the rescue attempt was also canceled. The U.S. Secretary of War

Royal Lee at his Mankato home in 1997. Photograph by Neale Van Ness for the _St. Paul Pioneer Press_.

refused to approve the dangerous mission, fearing Nazi retaliation against other POWs.

Did I Do Enough?

By January 1945, Soviet forces were closing in on Oflag 64. The POWs were marched some two hundred miles to the west. They joined thousands of civilian refugees trudging across a bitter, war-scarred winter landscape, sometimes living off the flesh of dead horses.

At a large camp south of Berlin, Oflag 64 POWs were thrown together with some twenty-five prisoners from many countries. In April, Russian troops overran the region and took control of the camp.

It quickly became apparent that this "liberation" did not mean immediate freedom for the Americans. The Soviets intended to exchange American POWs for numerous Russian soldiers in American hands who did not want to be sent home.

Lee didn't wait around to be used for trade. After two years as a rebellious prisoner of the Nazis, he finally made his escape from Soviet custody. When an American reconnaissance unit passed by, Lee and some fellow POWs scrambled over the barbed wire and were free at last.

Though proud of the secret war waged by World War II POWs, Lee dismisses any suggestion that he suffered or contributed more than any American soldier who saw combat service in any war. In fact, Lee says one of the benefits of the war along the barbed-wire front was that it soothed the "little guilt complex" POWs suffered over having allowed themselves to be captured.

"You wondered sometimes: Did I really do my job? Did I do enough? Could I have done more?"

POWs, Lee says, needed ways of continuing the fight.

"A lot of guys got killed, you know."

Veda Ponikvar in 1989 at the *Free Press* office, sporting a poster for the movie that brought fleeting fame to the editor and the town of Chisholm. Photograph by Craig Borck for the *St. Paul Pioneer Press*.

The Voice of the Range

One warm Friday afternoon in the late 1970s, Veda Ponikvar was working alone in the storefront office of the *Chisholm Free Press.* She saw two men approaching the front door, and for a moment she was puzzled.

When you've been a small-town newspaper publisher and editor for decades, as Ponikvar had, you know just about everybody. These visitors were clearly not from Chisholm or anywhere else on Minnesota's Iron Range.

The men introduced themselves and said they were researching a book. They wondered if by any chance Ponikvar knew a man named Archibald Graham.

Doctor Graham was dead, Ponikvar told them. But yes, she had known him. Everybody in Chisholm had known him. Everybody had loved him.

Doc Graham was a pillar, Ponikvar soon explained, in a generation of far-sighted community leaders who had helped the immigrant society of the Iron Range thrive despite the often harsh climatic and economic conditions of Minnesota's far northern frontier.

Ray Kinsella, one of Ponikvar's curious visitors that day, would soon write a popular fantasy novel, *Shoeless Joe,* that would later be made into an even more popular movie, *Field of Dreams.* His fable would bestow improbable fleeting fame on Chisholm, Graham, and Ponikvar.

"Veda Ponikvar is a woman of few words," Kinsella wrote in a passage portraying his visit to the newspaper. This is a debatable description of a woman who has written upward of five thousand outspoken opinion columns in more than half a century as a journalistic icon of northern Minnesota.

The novelist's eye was more accurate in perceiving the all-American romance and inspiring decency of the twentieth-century saga of Minnesota's mining region —a drama Veda Ponikvar, even more than Doc Graham, has epitomized and shaped.

Downtown Chisholm, 1920.
St. Paul Pioneer Press **file photo.**

All in the Same Cauldron

Ponikvar was born in Chisholm in 1919, the eldest of five children born to parents who hailed from Slovenia in eastern Europe, in what used to be Yugoslavia. She did not speak a word of English, she says, until she started kindergarten.

"And I wasn't the only one," Ponikvar adds, remembering an elementary school that must have resembled the Tower of Babel. There were students, she says, who spoke only Norwegian, only Swedish, only Finnish, only Italian, only Yiddish, only Polish, only Russian, and many more.

In the early years of the century, few places in the United States—probably only New York City—rivaled the kaleidoscopic cultural mixture and old-world atmosphere of Minnesota's Iron Range. About half the region's population was foreign born in 1910. The immigrants represented more than forty distinct ethnic groups.

Ponikvar's family, on both sides, had arrived on the Range during the period of the great migration, from 1890 to the start of World War I in 1914. That quarter century saw the swiftest concentrated resettlement of human beings in history, with some fifteen million Europeans emigrating to the United States (especially, in those years, from southern and eastern Europe).

By 1910, nearly eighty thousand people lived on Minnesota's Iron Range. There, in the 1880s, the world's greatest deposit of high-grade iron ore had been discovered in what was otherwise a beautiful but remote and forbidding wilderness of deep forests and interminable winters.

Ponikvar notes that such legendary pioneers of the iron mining industry as Charlemagne Tower and the Merritt brothers vigorously recruited immigrants to move to the Range, especially from the Slavic countries and Scandinavia. Some of those groups had mining backgrounds; all were accustomed to backbreaking work for stingy pay.

The iron barons may also have had a self-serving reason for welcoming what we would today call a diverse workforce—miners of many nationalities and religions speaking many different languages. (Something called "Mine English" quickly evolved as a common tongue for essential communications at work.)

It was not lost on the bosses that ethnic and religious divisions and communication barriers made organizing mine workers into unions much more difficult.

The social fragmentation among ethnic groups may have helped encourage the

Miners' housing, near Chisholm, about 1910. In the Iron Range immigrant community, said a missionary, "the old line of Constantine" went right down the center of roads and boardinghouse tables. *St. Paul Pioneer Press file photo.*

remarkable proliferation on the Range of saloons—which were not scarce, to be sure, anywhere in America in those days. An Immigration Commission report in 1909 found 356 saloons in fifteen Iron Range towns, probably because each community needed at least one for each significant ethnic group.

A Presbyterian missionary noted that "the old line of Constantine [dividing Catholics and Orthodox Christians from eastern Europe] went right down the middle of a road, and sometimes right through the middle of a boardinghouse table."

Still, Ponikvar does not remember growing up in an atmosphere of suspicion. "There was no bitterness," she says. "We were all in the same cauldron. People were Italian, Jewish, Finn, Slovenian, Croat, Serb, whatever, and there was respect for each other. We appreciated each other. The rivalries didn't cross over here. I think that's the greatness of America and our democracy."

At the same time, the close-knit ethnic communities provided a warm, cooperative sense of security. "Our childhood was very beautiful," Ponikvar says. "There was a togetherness."

She remembers frequent "gatherings in the homes" for weddings and christenings and for no special reason at all on Sunday afternoons.

"Somebody would come with an accordion. There was always fresh baked bread and pastries on the table. We kids would play outside or sit in the corner watching the dances.

"The whole community pulled together," Ponikvar remembers. "Neighbors helped build barns and sheds and chicken coops. Mothers had their babies at home, and the doctor would come there, and neighbors took care of the other children. They'd stay for a few days or a week or whatever was needed."

Ponikvar's father was an underground miner. He loved the exhausting work, even though the erratic boom-and-bust cycles of the mining economy often impoverished his family. He was also an avid newspaper reader, fascinated with politics and public affairs and devoted to American democracy. Increasingly, as the years went by, he became a loyal but pragmatic union man.

In all these ways he profoundly influenced his eldest daughter.

"I can remember he would sit at the dining-room table and read all the newspapers—the Slovenian ones and the English ones. He'd come home from the mine, his boots and clothes covered with ore dust, and mother would have dinner ready. He'd finish eating, change clothes, and leave for night school."

Those were the years of the "Americanization" movement. Immigration was restricted after 1924, and newer arrivals were pushed and helped to learn English, become American citizens, and adopt American ideas and customs. Under laws in effect at the time, Ponikvar's mother, who had been born in Ely of Slovenian immigrant parents, lost her citizenship when she married a noncitizen. She too attended night school to become naturalized.

Workers made only slow progress improving their conditions before World War II. The depression of the 1930s hit the Range especially hard. Mine wages remained under one dollar an hour as late as the mid-1940s. Union agitation did inspire mining companies beginning in the 1920s to improve safety in the mines and offer educational and health-care services in the Range communities.

Ponikvar remembers mostly a spirit of "tenacity," "drive," and "cohesiveness" during her youth in Chisholm. That "cradle of people of many tongues and creeds," as she has called it, benefited from exceptional leadership, she says, including beloved mayors and school officials.

One of the community's leaders was Doc Graham, a North Carolinian who answered an ad for a position in Chisholm after his brief baseball career ended, and never left. His competence, charity, and dedication turned his "simple, humble" existence into "a Life of Greatness," as Ponikvar was to write in an obituary that would find its way into Kinsella's novel and movie.

"These people," Ponikvar says of Rangers, "then and now are survivors, very resilient. They feel that they live in the greatest country in the world, a country worth defending."

Unreal

In December of 1941, "the sky fell in," Ponikvar says, with the Japanese attack on Pearl Harbor and America's entry into World War II. The next year, after graduating from Drake University with a journalism degree, Ponikvar became editor of the *Chisholm Tribune Herald*. With so many men off to war, the unusual opportunity became available to a woman.

But while running a newspaper in her hometown was her dream, Ponikvar just then felt called to defend America. She is quick to note the Iron Range's crucial contribution to America's war effort, in the form of some ninety million tons of iron ore mined on average each year during the conflict, iron that became the ships, planes, and tanks that overwhelmed Germany and Japan.

After five months, Ponikvar quit the newspaper and enlisted in the navy. Her knowledge of Slavic languages and culture earned her an assignment with Naval Intelligence in Washington, D.C. Soon she was heading the Yugoslav, Polish, and Czech desks.

Even today, Ponikvar is somewhat circumspect about discussing her intelligence work. It involved receiving and analyzing reports of ship deployments and other military information, mainly in and around Yugoslavia. Poland and Czechoslovakia, overrun by Germany early in the war, saw little action.

But Yugoslavia was a bloody battleground. The various Yugoslav ethnic groups that made so much heartbreaking news in the 1990s—Serbs, Croats, Bosnians, Slovenians—battled each other as well as the Nazis and the Soviets throughout World War II. The region suffered, all at once, "a civil war, revolution, interregional skirmishes, and a global war," Ponikvar says. "It was unreal." Today's animosities in the Balkans owe much to that bitter era.

Some of the best sources of intelligence information, Ponikvar says, were right in Washington. Other sources included battlefield correspondents, who would call on intelligence offices when they returned to the states and share what they knew. Among the famed reporters the aspiring journalist was thrilled to befriend were Edward R. Murrow and Harry Reasoner.

Like many Americans who lived through World War II, Ponikvar remembers the great crusade fondly. "I wouldn't trade those four years for all the money in the world," she says. "The experience, the contacts, the knowledge that was shared."

But at war's end, she knew she wanted to go home.

Benevolent Dictator

"I love Minnesota," Ponikvar says. "I love the Range. The four seasons. The diversity of culture, of heritage, of language. The fantastic work ethic."

There is in Ponikvar's feeling for her home something of the sentiment novelist Kinsella put in the mouth of Doc Graham's ghost: "Once the land touches you," he says, "the wind never blows so cold again."

In 1947, Ponikvar borrowed money and founded the biweekly *Chisholm Free Press*. It was virtually unheard of at the time for a woman to undertake such a venture. Skepticism was predictable.

"They said she'll go broke in six weeks," Ponikvar recalls. "Then it was three months. Then six months. Then a year. And then it stopped."

Instead, by 1955, Ponikvar was in a position to buy the town's competing paper, becoming the undisputed journalistic voice of Chisholm and the Iron Range.

No mere detached observer, she soon became exactly the kind of strong-willed, community-spirited leader she had admired so much in the Chisholm of her youth. In fact, she may have set a new standard for influence, becoming what a Chisholm-area writer calls the "benevolent dictator" of the town, if not the region.

An outspoken member of the Democratic-Farmer-Labor Party, Ponikvar offered advice—sometimes solicited and sometimes not, but rarely ignored—to generations of politicians, from Hubert Humphrey to Walter Mondale to Congressman

James Oberstar. They in turn have relied on her to monitor and massage the mood of constituents on the Range.

Such direct hands-on involvement in politics and community affairs is no longer the fashion among journalists. But Ponikvar, who makes no apologies, might counter that it is also no longer the fashion for doctors to dispense charity or for neighbors to come to one another in need.

Ponikvar, at all events, was in the thick of every major political struggle that concerned the Iron Range in the twentieth century's second half. She fought for the 1964 taconite amendment that secured tax advantages to help build the taconite industry. She was instrumental in the effort to grant federal wilderness protection to the Boundary Waters Canoe Area. She pushed for the establishment of the Iron World center, which preserves the history of the Range and its peoples, and for Northwest Airlines' investment in a reservations center in Chisholm. She is among the founders of an institution for the developmentally disabled in Chisholm.

The Chisholm fire depart-
ment shows off its gear,
1920. *St. Paul Pioneer Press*
file photo.

: 129 :

Selected statistics from Minnesota's Iron Range:	1910	1942	1979	1994
Millions of tons of ore mined	35.1	75.4	60.2	43.9
Minnesota production as percent of U.S. total	61%	71%	86%	76%
Mining employees	17,320	13,705	14,462	6,051
Average mine wages per hour	$0.33	$0.88	$8.85	$11.75
Fatal injuries	78	14	0	1
Total Iron Range population	77,655	96,950	106,870 (1980)	90,865 (1990)
Iron Range population as percent of Minnesota total	3.9%			1.9%

Sources: **U.S. Bureau of the Census,** Statistical Abstract **and** Historical Statistics**; calculations of Professor Arnold Alanen, University of Wisconsin-Madison;** Reports to the Inspector of Mines, Itasca, St. Louis, and Crow Wing Counties.

"Everybody knew where I stood," Ponikvar says of her thousands of twice-weekly commentaries in her newspaper. She continues to write them, along with news stories, even though she finally sold the paper in 1995. The new owners soon asked her to resume her contributions.

It is still not difficult to discover where Ponikvar stands. It is usually with Democrats, workers, and the interests of her region. And yet, inheriting her father's cautious union sensibilities, she argues that a balance is needed between labor and management and that "strikes don't solve anything."

Her patriotism and military background made the Vietnam War era "very difficult" for Ponikvar. "I stood my ground," she says. She decried war protesters' undermining of the presidential campaign of Hubert Humphrey and called for respect for the military and troops in combat. She fumes over reports today of homeless Vietnam veterans. "That should not be," she says simply. "It's wrong."

Ponikvar believes American society has taken a misguided "permissive" turn in recent decades, depleting many of its sources of strength. The weakening of family ties and the increase in divorce bother her because "that unity of family, that cohesiveness, that was the thing that opened the great north road, that opened the west. We don't have the tenacity, drive, and loyalty to do the right thing today. There's an element missing."

Ponikvar herself never married. But she came close, she says, with a navy man, of Slovenian descent, who died of cancer in 1976. Admitting she's made "sacrifices" to live out her dream, she adds, "I've never been sorry."

Of Doc Graham, Ponikvar wrote, "His era was historic. There will never be another quite like it."

It was Ponikvar's era, too.

While Minnesota iron mining has surely seen its glory days, Iron Range communities may enjoy a satisfactory future as centers for more diversified economies. But the passing from prominence of such figures as Veda Ponikvar marks the disappearance of a uniquely colorful, energetic, and optimistic society that appeared as abruptly as a summer storm in Minnesota's north woods.

"Those of us who have experienced all these things," Ponikvar says, "have an obligation to tell the story."

Jim Griffin, future deputy police chief, in curls, about 1922.
Photograph courtesy of Jim Griffin.

Discrimination and Progress

"Stand in one of the squares marked on the floor," barked the naval officer. "In each square you'll find a cardboard box with a label. Write your address on the label, stick it on the box, and fill the box with your clothes. They'll be shipped home."

It was spring 1945. Jim Griffin was among the disrobing recruits being inducted into the U.S. Navy at the Great Lakes Naval Base near Chicago.

"While I'm standing there," Griffin remembers, "a young sailor came over and looked at me and said, 'Are you colored?'

"I said, 'Are you blind?'"

Not blind. Just following regulations. The roster of inductees the sailor was checking listed Griffin's name right along with the rest. But in the segregated navy of that era, blacks were supposed to be listed on a form separate from whites. Among some one hundred inductees that day, Griffin was the only black recruit.

Says Griffin: "I told him, 'One sheet for everybody is just the way they do it up in Minnesota.'"

Up in Minnesota, Griffin, then twenty-eight, was a patrolman with the St. Paul Police Department. He'd gotten into law enforcement not because he had a special zeal for police work, but because he needed a job. Jobs had been desperately hard to come by for years, especially if you were black.

In time, Griffin would become a history-making officer, the first African American to achieve high rank on the St. Paul force. His final promotion, to deputy chief, would come only after a well-publicized discrimination dispute.

In 1972, Griffin, by then a captain, scored number one on the qualifying test for deputy chief. "They're always saying minorities can't pass tests," Griffin says. "I never did agree with that."

Jim Griffin at his St. Paul home in 1997. Photograph by Carolyn Kaster for the *St. Paul Pioneer Press*.

But the police chief, Richard Rowan, chose to pass over Griffin for the second-ranked candidate, who happened to be white. Griffin challenged the decision, as Twin Cities civil-rights organizations and others denounced the department's bias.

In the end, the city created not one but two deputy chief positions, so promotions could be given to both Griffin and his rival, William McCutcheon, who, in 1980, became police chief.

Griffin considers his elevation to deputy chief "the highlight of my career." Many observers consider it a landmark victory over discrimination in the Twin Cities.

For Griffin, it was nothing new.

We Don't Hire Colored People Here

Griffin was born in St. Paul in 1917 on Rondo Avenue. "I've always been kind of a plugger for St. Paul," he says. "For just living, for a black person, this is as good a place as you're ever going to find."

Griffin remembers the St. Paul of his youth as "an ethnic town," where poor Italians, poor Jews, poor Irish, and other minority groups shared the struggles, and often the neighborhoods, of African Americans. "Wherever there's poor people, you find blacks," Griffin says.

St. Paul's black population was so small in those years before the depression that there was little tension, Griffin says—or at least less than people today imagine there was.

Black Minnesota history has long been Griffin's hobby, and he eagerly dispels many myths about early twentieth-century St. Paul.

"I read an article once," he says, "written by a black person, that said blacks couldn't skate at the Hollow Rink in those days." Yet the popular, block-square rink west of downtown "was where I learned to skate," Griffin says. "All the black kids learned to skate there.

"I read another article that said they didn't allow blacks to live west of Lexington. I could name twenty-five black families that lived west of Lexington."

Exaggerations of historic restrictions thrive, Griffin thinks, because many southern blacks who migrated north in later years to such places as St. Paul were disappointed because they "thought they were coming to utopia."

It was hardly utopia. Griffin remembers how housing discrimination and residential segregation increased sharply as the African American population gradually increased in the 1920s. He remembers, too, how job opportunities, always severely limited for blacks, all but vanished when the depression hit.

Jim with his mother, Lorena, about 1927. When his father died five years later, in the depths of the depression, Griffin would embark on a long, hard search for opportunity in a society hostile to black aspirations. Photograph courtesy of Jim Griffin.

Griffin's father had been a dining-car waiter for the Northern Pacific railroad. Griffin says such "servant jobs" for railroads and hotels were "the backbone of black employment" in the early part of the century.

At the time, there were not large numbers of white women seeking such work. But with the hardships of the depression, white females and males alike sought any kind of job, and black waiters were routinely fired to make room for them. Black unemployment during the depression frequently topped 60 percent.

Griffin's father died in 1932, just as the depression hit bottom. In 1936, fresh out of high school, Griffin began his search for opportunity.

African American population, as percentage of total:	1900	1950	Today
Minnesota	0.3	0.4	2.4
St. Paul	1.4	1.8	7.4
Minneapolis	0.7	1.3	13.0

Source: U.S. Bureau of the Census. The "Today" column shows the most recent figures available at time of writing.

He recalls walking into the Hamm's Brewery office that summer to ask about a job.

"We don't hire colored people here," he was told, matter-of-factly.

Twin Cities breweries were the target of antidiscrimination boycotts by black consumers in those years. But it was not until after World War II that hiring bans against blacks were lifted at many Twin Cities businesses.

For two full years in the late 1930s, Griffin could find no steady work. In 1939, when the St. Paul police and fire departments announced qualifying exams, he was one of 1,200 men who took the tests.

He did well. But a prehiring physical turned up an unexpected chemical problem in Griffin's urine that disqualified him. His own doctor tested him and found nothing wrong. Twice more, Griffin went back for tests; twice more, the department found disqualifying problems.

Griffin suspected skin color, not urine chemistry, was his real affliction. He played his last card. He paid a call on a St. Paul City Council member, Axel Peterson Sr., whose son had been a schoolmate of Griffin. He told Peterson how he was being "horsed around." Peterson promised to speak with someone.

"And lo and behold," Griffin says, "all my physical problems cleared up." Griffin was sworn in as a St. Paul police recruit on August 6, 1941.

Within months, America entered World War II. Still going through part-time police training, Griffin sought a moonlighting guard job at the Federal Cartridge Corporation's Twin City Ordnance Plant, then gearing up for war production. He got "a lot of crap" when he first tried to apply. But he persevered and became the first black employed at the plant in more than a janitorial role.

Before the war was over, the plant would employ more than one thousand African Americans, one-fifth of the state's adult black population. It was a critical employment breakthrough for Minnesota blacks.

Indignities

Before the war was over, Griffin had become a navy recruit, explaining to a confused young clerk that he was, indeed, "colored," whatever the paperwork suggested.

As soon as his race was settled, Griffin was ordered to report to a small room where he found several sailors "with a big bucket, with a lot of gooey crap in it, and paintbrushes."

"The guy said, 'Drop your shorts.'

"I said, 'For what?'

"He said, 'We're going to paint you up for crabs. We do it to all the black guys who come through here.'

The Griffin family in 1950, when Jim ran unsuccessfully for the Minnesota legislature. From left: Vianne, Edna, Jim, Helen, and Linda. Vianne died in 1973. A scholarship named for her is given each year at St. Paul Central High School. Photograph courtesy of Jim Griffin.

Patrolman Griffin examines a recovered stolen safe, about 1954. *St. Paul Pioneer Press* file photo.

"Those are the kinds of indignities you had to go through. It made you madder than hell."

Griffin had a reason for facing the indignities the military reserved for black recruits. Married with two small children and employed in essential work, he was exempt from the wartime draft. Yet he'd finally taken a friend's advice and enlisted because Minnesota, then as now, had one of the country's strongest "veteran's preference" laws in public employment. Winning promotion in the police department without veteran status seemed unlikely. And Griffin planned to win some promotions.

It was a struggle all the way. Griffin remembers especially well one comment that got back to him while he was trying for his first promotion, to sergeant. A white cop had been overheard confidently reassuring others: "They'll never make a nigger the boss on this job."

The first black patrolman had joined the St. Paul Police Department in 1881. Griffin became the department's first black sergeant in 1955. He became its first black captain in 1970; and finally, two years later, he became its first black deputy chief. He was subsequently elected four times to the St. Paul School Board, the second black member ever.

Anywhere else but comparatively tolerant Minnesota, Griffin believes, his "problems with discrimination would have been worse."

He notes, too, that the police department was integrated earlier than many institutions. He says he remembers no black reporters at the *St. Paul Pioneer Press* when he joined the police force in 1941. (In fact, there were none until the early 1970s.)

None of Griffin's later successes was certain, or even particularly probable, in 1945.

"Madder than hell," Griffin resisted the sailors with their gooey buckets and their orders to treat all black recruits for crabs.

"I said, 'Hell, I ain't got any crabs! There ain't nothing wrong with me!'

"Finally, another guy asked me, 'Where the hell are you from?'

"I said Minnesota, and he said: 'Aw, hell. Them guys up there don't have all those problems. Let him go through.'"

SS General Ernst Kaltenbrunner, apprehended by Bob Matteson at war's end and hanged at Nuremberg. He "wrote his name in blood," prosecutors said. Photograph courtesy of Jane Matteson.

Wars Hot and Cold

Few Americans who lived through 1968 will ever forget the jarring climax year of the troubled 1960s.

Arguably the most traumatic twelve months for America in the twentieth century's second half, 1968 saw the assassinations of presidential candidate Robert Kennedy and civil-rights leader Martin Luther King Jr. King's murder and other grievances set a dozen American cities ablaze that year with race riots.

The Democratic National Convention in August, where Minnesotans Hubert Humphrey and Eugene McCarthy battled for the presidential nomination, was rocked and scarred by violent street battles between Chicago police and Vietnam War protesters. During the same month, Soviet tanks crushed a liberalization movement in Czechoslovakia, and the cold war raged on.

So did a hot war in Vietnam. The traumas of 1968 had begun with conviction on January 30 with the Tet Offensive. It was the boldest direct attack Vietnamese communists launched against American forces in the entire war. A simultaneous guerrilla assault struck hundreds of cities and villages in South Vietnam, America's ally in the war. Though it achieved no real military success, Tet's scale and bloodiness shocked America and strengthened antiwar sentiment.

No American was more shocked and alarmed on the morning of January 30, 1968, than St. Paul native Jane Matteson, then living in Washington, D.C. Early reports on Tet indicated that the fighting had begun in the South Vietnamese city of Nha Trang.

Nha Trang was where Jane's husband, Bob, was stationed. He was director of civilian affairs in the central region of South Vietnam. In charge of CIA, State Department, and other civilian staff, Bob was running America's "pacification" program in that region. The effort's purpose, in the memorable phrase of the time, was to win the battle for the "hearts and minds" of the South Vietnamese peasantry.

The villagers were also persistently wooed and intimidated by communist guerrillas, the Viet Cong.

Bob's occupation seemed more than usually hazardous as Jane heard reports of Viet Cong fighters popping up from the sewers of Nha Trang and other South Vietnamese cities.

"Naturally," Jane remembers, "I was quite frantic, to the point of losing all reason and calling Stan Resor, Secretary of the Army. It was ridiculous. The Tet Offensive had just happened, and the whole world was collapsing around his ears. But I called and said, 'How's Bob doing?'

"Stan said, 'Gee, I don't know. I haven't talked to him just lately. But I'll find out and get back to you.'"

The remarkable twentieth-century adventure of Jane and Bob Matteson had begun in St. Paul's fashionable Hill District. Born two years and several blocks apart on Lincoln Avenue during World War I, the fortunate youngsters knew each other "vaguely" growing up. Jane's memories of Bob in those years are only that

Jane and Bob Matteson on their wedding day, 1940. A year later, an extraordinary twentieth-century adventure would begin with America's entry into World War II. Photograph courtesy of Jane Matteson.

she "never liked him," thinking the star athlete at St. Paul Academy (and later Carleton College) was just "a big jock."

Later, Jane says, Bob "became my hero, when I realized he had a soul. He was very good at everything. The only thing I ever did that he didn't do was I became eighty. He died at seventy-eight."

Bob "checked out," as Jane often puts it, in 1994, suffering from Parkinson's disease. "I hate to have him gone," she says. But she adds that the avid canoeist and mountain climber "was not the kind of person" to have a wasting disease. "It was a big drag for him."

They had married in 1940. Soon, World War II was "rumbling," Jane says, and Bob enlisted.

"The war years seemed very long," Jane remembers. "When the fifth-year anniversary came around, and we realized how short it had actually been, I couldn't believe it."

Weekly during the war, Jane would join a group of soldiers' wives and older couples that would gather at a Summit neighborhood home, have a potluck lunch, and "sing seriously—seriously." Mastering complex choral works seemed to help pass the frightening war years.

They were years when "every little once in a while, a good friend of yours would get killed," Jane recalls.

Meanwhile, Bob was approaching what he would later call "the most memorable event" of an adventurous life.

Good Hunting

It was May—a glorious, fragrant May in the Austrian Alps. Bob was having trouble keeping his mind on his work. A "rushing mountain stream cascaded merrily . . . its spray sparkling in the early morning sun," he wrote in a memoir. "Above us and all around us were snow-capped peaks, and on the green-covered Alps were brilliant displays of brightly colored mountain flowers."

It was a grim business Matteson was struggling to concentrate on. It was May 1945. He was Nazi hunting in the last stronghold of the Third Reich. The hunting was good.

Adolf Hitler's dreadful war machine, which had swept all Europe before it only five years earlier, had collapsed with surprising speed in World War II's final months. By late spring, the führer had died a coward's death by his own hand. The last mad scheme of the Nazi leaders had failed to materialize.

That scheme was the "Alpenfestung"—the Alpine Fortress. If all else failed, the Nazi warlords had planned to retreat to a complex of bunkers and ammunition dumps they had installed amid the jagged, forbidding peaks of western Austria. There, they would make one final, bloody stand.

That last battle was never fought. But the Alpenfestung region was nonetheless crawling with Nazi chieftains when Special Agent Bob Matteson arrived in the four-thousand-person village of Alt Aussee on May 9. He was in command of a Counter Intelligence Corps team attached to the 80th Infantry Division of General George Patton's Third Army.

Matteson learned later that Adolf Eichmann had fled the far end of Alt Aussee just as the Americans had arrived. The officer in charge of the "final solution" that exterminated six million European Jews, Eichmann would continue to elude justice until 1960. That year, Israeli secret agents kidnapped Eichmann in Argentina and took him back to Israel, where he was tried and hanged.

Eichmann's boss was at the top of Matteson's arrest list. He was SS General Ernst Kaltenbrunner, chief of the Gestapo and commandant of the entire Nazi police and spy apparatus. An intimate of Hitler, Kaltenbrunner supervised the Holocaust and innumerable Nazi war crimes. He is believed to have occasionally used concentration camp inmates for target practice.

"He wrote his name in blood," a prosecutor at the Nuremberg war crimes trial later declared of Kaltenbrunner, "a name to be remembered as a symbol for cruelty, degradation and death."

On May 11, after pursuing various leads for days, Matteson received a tip from a local resistance leader that Kaltenbrunner might be found holed up at a primitive mountain chalet, a five-hour climb from Alt Aussee into the remote, snow-packed high country. Matteson immediately recruited four ex-Nazi soldiers as guides. Accompanied by an infantry squad, they started climbing at midnight.

Snowslides and washed-out bridges added hazard and hardship to the patrol's tense, dark trek. Often, they struggled through snow up to their knees. Dawn was just brightening when they reached the ramshackle cabin.

In a local civilian costume, complete with "lederhosen and spiked shoes," Matteson approached the cabin alone, hoping to surprise Kaltenbrunner and take him alive.

Waking a guard, Matteson handed him a note. A few days before, Matteson had found Kaltenbrunner's mistress, Gisela Von Westarp, and had persuaded her to write a message for her lover. It pleaded with Kaltenbrunner to give himself up to the disguised American agent who had tracked him down.

The guard read this note and disappeared inside the cabin. For a few long minutes, it looked as if Kaltenbrunner and his men were preparing to make a fight of it. Then, they abruptly walked out on the cabin's porch with their hands raised.

The Nazi general had hatched one last, far-fetched plan. He would claim that he had long before turned against Hitler, and for years had been secretly working for the Reich's defeat.

It was another scheme that failed. Tried by the International Military Tribunal at Nuremberg, Kaltenbrunner was one of eleven top Nazis condemned to death and hanged.

Matteson's Silver Star citation for gallantry concluded:

> *Special Agent Matteson's careful planning and fearless execution of a dangerous mission against an armed enemy of the most vicious and desperate type are a credit to himself and to the Armed Forces of the United States. Entered military service from Minnesota.*

The Way I Used to Feel

A new spirit of ambition and idealism reigned after the war, Jane Matteson says. Financially, the Mattesons were lucky, "a little bit independent," Jane says. Bob soon embarked on a public life, becoming a political researcher and an aide to Harold Stassen, who became a profound influence on the Mattesons' lives.

Bob Matteson with naturalist Sigurd Olson while Matteson was running the Sigurd Olson Environmental Institute at Northland College in Cable, Wisconsin. Photograph courtesy of Jane Matteson.

Bob and Jane Matteson in
the late 1980s. Photograph
courtesy of Jane Matteson.

Stassen was a popular governor of Minnesota from 1939 to 1943. He founded a brand of moderate, reformist Republican politics that has been an important force in Minnesota and the nation ever since. An outspoken internationalist, he served as a delegate to the United Nations Charter Conference in 1945 and later as a cabinet-level foreign-policy adviser to President Eisenhower.

Stassen was a serious candidate for president several times in the 1940s and 1950s. Today, many people remember him mainly as a not-so-serious, perennial contender in later years.

Bob Matteson worked for Stassen in various capacities from 1946 to 1958, sharing Stassen's enthusiasm for arms control and international cooperation. The close, enduring friendship of Jane and Bob Matteson and Harold and Esther Stassen was called "one of the worthiest examples of friendship our state has ever seen," by former governor Elmer L. Andersen.

The work with Stassen took Jane and Bob, for extended periods, to Geneva, London, and elsewhere. But Jane, busy with five children, loved Washington best. Vassar-educated and "more of a social animal" than her husband, she found life in the nation's capital "endlessly fascinating. You never knew who you would see when you went out to dinner. There was always something going on."

The Kennedy era in the early 1960s, with its influx of younger people into Washington and its giddy sense of possibility, was especially exciting, Jane says. Even for Republicans.

"Well, not for *good* Republicans," she adds. "But we weren't *good* Republicans."

During and after his Vietnam service, Bob increasingly lost confidence in America's war policy, doubting the struggle could be won. Like a hundred million American families, the Mattesons had endured division with their own children over the war ("nothing fatal," Jane says).

By the end of Richard Nixon's first term, in 1972, Bob and Jane decided it was time to end their twenty-year Washington career, during which Bob had worked in foreign policy for every administration of both parties.

They moved to Cable, Wisconsin, where they had spent vacations ever since their youth. There, Bob helped establish the Sigurd Olson Environmental Institute at Northland College. For the next twenty years, travel and Bob's work on his voluminous memoirs rounded out a dramatically quieter life than the Mattesons had ever known.

They moved back to the Twin Cities in the early 1990s because of Bob's illness. Since his death in 1994, Jane has found opportunity in her new independence. She's discovered a "new addiction" to jazz music, which at its best (particularly old standards) has the power, Jane says, to make her "feel in my heart the way I used to feel." Jane has become a fixture and an icon at a popular St. Paul jazz club, the Dakota Bar and Grill. She's working to organize an educational program introducing schoolchildren to jazz.

Her new cause and passion "never would have happened," Jane says, "if my dear husband hadn't checked out. I hate to say that, but he never would have been willing to go out this often or stay up this late. I guess because of my age, I don't want to miss anything."

Three decades ago, on the day the Tet Offensive began, Jane waited fearfully, wondering if Secretary of the Army Stan Resor would or could actually call her back with news of Bob.

"He did call back, in about two hours, and said, 'He's fine. He's perfectly fine.' Stan couldn't have been nicer, acting as if he had all the time in the world."

The traumas of 1968 mark the beginning of a change in American political attitudes in the later twentieth century. Vietnam, the Watergate scandal soon to follow, public uneasiness with the size and cost of government, and much else have combined to produce a cynicism toward public service that Jane Matteson laments.

"There's nothing worse than saying my day was so much better. But it's true that there is less respect for government today than there used to be. All the while we were in Washington, people had a great respect for government.

"If you were in government service then, you were fortunate. People admired you for doing it."

Father Hans Jacobse at his Duluth church in 1997. Only in America, perhaps, could a Dutch immigrant at last find a cultural and philosophical home as a Greek Orthodox priest. Photograph by Joe Rossi for the *St. Paul Pioneer Press*.

"The Sixties"

"Wake up . . . wake up. We're coming to America this morning."

It was a misty March dawn in 1957. Hans Jacobse (JAKE-ub-see) was six years old and about to complete the first long journey of his life. The cramped cabin of the old immigrant ship swayed lazily, the way it had for ten long days at sea.

Jacobse's father shook the boy awake. He was to get up and come out on deck to watch for the Statue of Liberty.

"I didn't know what a 'Statue of Liberty' was," Jacobse remembers. "But when your dad says you have to go see this thing, you go see this thing."

On deck, immigrants were gathering near the bow of the ship, peering out into a patchy fog. Most were speaking quietly in a language Jacobse couldn't understand. The ship carried many Hungarians—refugees from a failed uprising the previous autumn against communist rule.

The Jacobses were from the Netherlands, and they, too, were refugees. They were among the last Europeans admitted to the United States under the War Refugee Act, as a result of hardship and dislocation during World War II.

Jacobse's father, Teunis, had been a forger for the Dutch underground resistance against Nazi occupation. Captured by the Germans, he was imprisoned in a concentration camp. He escaped in the final months of the war and lived off the land for three months as a fugitive.

Jacobse's mother, Tina, and her family were driven from their home by the Nazis. Resettled, they hid her brother from Nazi conscription in a concealed compartment behind a wall.

"They'd both had enough," Jacobse says of his parents' restlessness, which persisted and propelled them to emigrate more than a decade after the war ended. "Europe was tired, and America held great promise."

The future Father Jacobse in his mother's arms, in the Netherlands, about 1952. Photograph courtesy of Hans Jacobse.

As he shivered against the damp cold at the bow of the immigrant ship, young Jacobse understood only that something of importance was about to happen. The deck was crowded now with fellow passengers gazing out across the shrouded sea.

Suddenly Jacobse's father pointed and shouted: "There it is! There it is! There it is!"

The boy saw the statue, its uplifted torch, appearing and disappearing behind drifting wisps of fog. All around him the immigrants were pointing and talking excitedly.

"I didn't quite understand the importance of it all," Jacobse recalls. "And most of the people were speaking a language I didn't understand. But I could understand excitement."

Perhaps sensing his son's confusion, Jacobse's father bent down and said, "Remember this. Always remember this."

The son has remembered. "It's still very clear," Jacobse says of that murky morning in New York harbor. "I'm grateful to my father for this memory. It symbolizes for me coming to America. As an adult, I can understand what that means and what it meant for so many other immigrants.

"There were so many millions who came over so many years. And most didn't have the security we were offered. We had a sponsor and a place to live waiting for us. But so many had come in such poverty, from war-torn countries. Fleeing indescribable hardship and facing indescribable uncertainty. Yet full of hope.

"Where else but America could this happen?"

Just Like an American

It may be even more certain that Jacobse's second long journey could have unfolded "only in America." The patriotic Dutch immigrant is today a Greek Orthodox priest. From 1991 to 1997, Father Hans Jacobse served as a pastor at St. Mary's Greek Orthodox Church in Minneapolis and at Twelve Holy Apostles Greek Orthodox Church in Duluth. He now runs a home for children in New York.

After landing in New York back in 1957, the Jacobse family traveled directly to Minneapolis. Parishioners from Hennepin Avenue Methodist Church, the family's sponsor, moved them into a suburban rental home. "And the next day," Jacobse says, "life in America began."

Yet American life began, Jacobse remembers, "in a culturally European home." Unlike many other immigrants before and since, the Jacobses had not come to America with a large wave of compatriots who formed a close-knit immigrant community within the new society. They were, to that extent, unusually isolated.

"Especially in those first years," Jacobse remembers, "there was a strong sense that the Americans were different than we were. When my mother would get angry with us kids, the first thing she'd say was, 'You're acting just like an American. Now stop it!' It was selfish behavior that made her say that."

Jacobse and his siblings learned English rapidly, within months, from neighborhood children. His father spoke English well, but his mother spoke only Dutch. For years, Jacobse translated for his mother at stores and with neighbors.

In the early 1960s, the Jacobses settled in the Twin Cities suburb of Eden Prairie. It was there, as a fifth-grader, that Jacobse heard for the first time about a small war in a distant place called Vietnam.

He remembers thinking: "Oh, I don't have to worry about that. That will be over before I'm older."

The Jacobse family, soon after arriving in America, about 1957. Hans is standing in front of his mother, Tina, for whom he and the other children soon began translating. Photograph courtesy of Hans Jacobse.

Instead, Vietnam and the cultural upheaval of the 1960s would transform and traumatize Jacobse's generation and leave the immigrant feeling more rootless than ever.

Jacobse remembers the 1960s as "a time of tremendous dislocation" for young Americans. "Deep questions were thrust upon us before we had the resources or experience to answer them," he says.

The social and political turmoil of the '60s had many causes. Excruciating controversies over civil rights and Vietnam helped radicalize a huge and restless postwar baby-boom generation. Mainstream society was confronted with fundamental doubts about American life and values that had long been debated mainly in intellectual circles and among political radicals.

"Everything was up for grabs," the way Jacobse remembers it. Capitalism, marriage, America's moral position in the world—all were skeptically questioned. Traditional religious faith was widely rejected even as youth eagerly sought transcendent truth in the drug culture and an almost cultlike devotion to rock music.

Vietnam lay at the center of what Jacobse perceived as "moral confusion." Like millions of young Americans, he was "afraid of going over there. But the worst was that the nation was of two minds about whether the war was right or wrong. Not just kids. The nation's leaders were of two minds."

Looking back, Jacobse believes much of the '60s youth rebellion was a search for some sort of "clarity" amid America's crisis of self-doubt. He suspects he per-

Jacobse was attending the University of Minnesota when Vietnam War protests led to the barricading of streets and violent clashes with police. The tensions and uncertainties of the era were especially confusing for the immigrant. Photographs by D. J. Tice.

sonally became "horribly obnoxious," defiant at school and at home, "pressing anyone in authority very, very hard."

"I was looking for something certain behind the authority," Jacobse says. "I implicitly trusted in authority. I think we all do. But there has to be a conviction behind the authority. I wasn't looking for absolute answers. I was looking for certainty in people."

But certainty was hard to find, at least among traditional sources of authority. Antiwar demonstrations turned violent on college campuses across the nation, including, in 1972, the University of Minnesota, where Jacobse was by then enrolled.

Unlike many of his peers, Jacobse says he found little solace or sense of community in the rock music culture. There was an "inner chaos," for him, in the playful mob hysteria of '60s rock concerts, in the way rock stars were idolized.

Jacobse believes the spiritual chaos of those years troubled many of his contemporaries. But he suspects he "felt it deeper," partly because he was an immigrant.

"Even when you come over as young as six years old, it's still an adopted culture," he says. "I embrace this life, this culture. I'm an American. But there's always a certain distance."

By the early 1970s, even though the Vietnam War ended, Jacobse's "distance"—his estrangement from both America's doubt-ridden traditional culture and the chaotic counterculture—produced "an acute personal crisis of the deepest dimension."

Sense of Wonder

It was a spiritual crisis. "My main polemical sparring partners had often been Christians at school," Jacobse remembers. "I loved to beat them down with my arguments. But I found their certainty appealing."

In the grip of his personal crisis, Jacobse "decided I had to find God. I had to put away the drugs, put away the moral confusion, and leave my friends and my life behind. I don't think most people have to do that. But I had to."

Despite unusual elements in his background and his urgings, Jacobse's spiritual wandering became in many ways an archetypal '60s generation quest. He hitchhiked to the West Coast, with no particular destination in mind, along interstate highways crawling in those years with confused and idealistic young searchers.

One Sunday afternoon, in Berkeley, California, while trudging along a street looking for a freeway entrance ramp not already overrun with fellow hitchhikers, Jacobse experienced what he calls "a deep conversion."

"God touched me," Jacobse says. That "touch" turned the immigrant's journey onto a new and unlikely course.

Soon Jacobse settled in with a Christian commune in Oregon. It was another emblematic '60s "scene" with a twist. The group Jacobse joined for several years taught traditional Protestant theology and practical living. "I learned how to work, how to support myself," Jacobse says. "And I got some rest."

By the late '70s, Jacobse was back in Minnesota, studying history at the university. More at peace but still searching for something he couldn't define, he first became intrigued with Orthodox Christianity through the work of Aleksandr Solzhenitsyn, the great Russian writer and dissident who in the 1970s was exiled to America by the Soviet communist regime.

Solzhenitsyn's critique of the extreme secularism of modern America described for Jacobse the moral confusion that had long troubled him.

"I asked myself, where does this man get his insight? What well is he drawing from?" The well, Jacobse learned, was Orthodox Christianity.

Not long after that, Jacobse met Susan Oberg, a practicing Greek Orthodox. In time they married, and in still more time, following a year at Princeton Seminary, Jacobse decided to convert to the Orthodox faith. After jointly managing a youth program for several years at a Minneapolis Greek Orthodox church, the Jacobses decided that Hans should become a priest. (In Orthodox Christianity, married men can become priests.) He was ordained in 1991.

Through his ministry in the Greek church, the Dutch immigrant has finally found a spiritual and cultural home in America. For Jacobse, Orthodoxy offers a remedy to the severe separation of the sacred and the everyday that he believes blinds modern America to the holiness of all of life. "Faith has to speak to the real stuff of life," he says. "I think Orthodoxy does."

The conflicts and crises of his own '60s youth fuel Jacobse's special interest in working with children, hoping to give them more clarity and guidance than he thinks his generation got.

"I try to give children courage," he says, "to be people of integrity. Children are starved for that today. Because ultimately they want to find themselves, and you can't find yourself without integrity."

Asked to look back through the fog of time to find a confused child standing on the bow of a ship, Jacobse says: "I still feel like that little boy. I remember that day because my father told me to remember it. But I also remember because it sparked my sense of wonder.

"The priesthood has restored that sense."

The Tet Offensive of 1968 brought devastation to the cities and villages of South Vietnam. It began for Charlie Wolden what he calls the "undoing of character." Here, a Saigon street in ruins. Photograph from AP/Wide World Photos; reprinted with permission.

Vietnam, 1968

It was like the parting of the Red Sea, Charlie Wolden remembers. Thousands of panicked South Vietnamese civilians were streaming out of the ancient city of Hue (pronounced "way")—"humping it out of town with whatever they could carry on their backs," Wolden says. Mile after mile, the dazed refugees moved to either side of the road to make way for trucks carrying U.S. marines into the city.

It was February 1, 1968. The Tet Offensive had begun a few days earlier, when Viet Cong communist guerrillas and North Vietnamese Army troops simultaneously launched ferocious attacks in hundreds of cities and villages across South Vietnam. It was the bloodiest battle during America's involvement in the Vietnam War. Nowhere was the fighting fiercer than in Hue.

Wolden had never before seen anyone die.

"We plowed right through roadblocks of brush and debris," Wolden says. "As we got further into town, the dust clouds kept getting bigger. I could see muzzle flashes in the windows of buildings up ahead. Everybody in the trucks was shooting back. The sound was just deafening.

"We passed a tank that had crashed and gotten jammed up inside a building. We went around a jeep, all burned out with a dead guy hanging out of it. There were dead guys all over the sidewalks. Not long dead.

"The truck tipped over. I remember lying on the concrete feeling numb over my whole body. Bullets were pinging off the concrete all around me, and I told myself if I lay here, they'll think I'm dead and stop shooting at me.

"For whatever reason, it occurred to me that there was no music. All I could think about, laying there being shot at, was there's no music. No background music. This isn't a movie."

That night, Wolden wrote a letter home. Reading it over, he was frightened to see that his handwriting still looked like a child's. He tore the letter up, thinking, "I can't be a little kid anymore."

That month, he would turn nineteen.

America's Suicide Attempt

Wolden, of Frederic, Wisconsin, about sixty miles northeast of St. Paul, is today a mental-health counselor specializing in helping Vietnam War veterans. He has spent all the years since 1968 making a long journey back from Vietnam and its horrors, a journey back to personal wholeness and happiness, a journey to rediscover "the kid I was before I went."

Wolden was one of 2.6 million Americans who served in Vietnam, most of them between 1964 and 1973.

Some 58,000 Americans died in Vietnam; 154,000 were wounded. In the whole thirty-year struggle for control of Indochina (1945–75), more than 200,000 South Vietnamese soldiers died, along with at least 800,000 North Vietnamese fighters. Civilian casualties were similar, without counting postwar atrocities in Cambodia and elsewhere.

Indochina had been a poorly and harshly governed colony of France since the nineteenth century. After liberation from Japanese occupation during World War II, Indochina erupted in rebellion, led by communist-nationalist Ho Chi Minh. France abandoned the fight in 1954, but America took over.

"It's a mistake to look at Vietnam independent of the rest of the twentieth century," says Wolden, who, like many Vietnam War veterans, has made a study of the conflict's history.

The generation of Americans who had fought World War II was single-mindedly determined never to repeat the mistake of the 1930s—being too slow to oppose radical totalitarianism. America resisted free elections in Vietnam in the 1950s for fear communists would win. (Hitler, after all, was a "nationalist" who had initially been elected.) Steadily escalating American military involvement followed. Yet, the United States never mustered the total-war determination to prevail that its opponents in Vietnam possessed from first to last.

Bitter dissension over Vietnam worsened after the Tet Offensive, even though it was a military victory for America. President Lyndon Johnson decided not to seek reelection in 1968. Later, Vietnam War strife contributed to the paranoid Watergate misdeeds that ended in President Richard Nixon's resignation. Vietnam inspired confusion about America's proper role in the world, which in many ways continues today.

British historian Paul Johnson has termed Vietnam "America's suicide attempt."

For hundreds of thousands of veterans, such as Wolden, Vietnam is much more than history—more than a lost and dubious battle in the middle of America's long and largely victorious "cold war" against communism.

"Everything I am, everything I do, everything I believe is skewed and biased by Vietnam and that whole indescribable experience," Wolden says.

"This is the message I have for all the vets: You get to decide who you want to be."

But Wolden also likes to share a reminder he's read: "When a patrol goes forty miles in, it's forty miles back out."

As Old as Combat Itself

The fighting in Hue was street to street, house to house. It lasted a month. For many days, Wolden remembers, his marine unit was in "a doughnut," fighting outward. It was impossible to remove the wounded.

One day, Wolden was shot in the buttocks. At a battalion aid station, he walked through rows of "dead and wounded, who'd been lying there for days in the rain

A marine reaches out to help his comrade floundering in a South Vietnamese stream, 1968. Short tours of duty and casualties kept personnel coming and going in Vietnam, creating an unusually isolating experience for the combat troops. Photograph from AP/Wide World Photos; reprinted with permission.

Charlie Wolden in Okinawa,
1971. Photograph courtesy
of Charlie Wolden.

and the wet. The doctors were covered with blood. I felt ashamed to be coming in there with the little problem I had."

A year earlier, Wolden and several high school buddies had decided on a whim to enlist in the marines. They were "intrigued with the mystique of 'a few good men,'" Wolden says. Besides, "doing your hitch" in the military was "very normal" at the time.

Wolden had grown up in a large family on a small farm not far from Superior, Wisconsin. Though antiwar sentiment was spreading in America by the time he enlisted in 1967, Wolden says little of it had reached rural Wisconsin, where a high school kid's thoughts dwelled on "what's going to happen at the basketball game and the dance this Friday."

After a few weeks of combat, Wolden says, he had become someone else. "I was hard after Hue," he says. "In order to survive, you had to become this hard, cold, emotionally numb, ruthless person who did not feel guilt or remorse."

This "disassociation" and "undoing of character," Wolden says, "is as old as combat itself. . . . *The Iliad* is about that. *The Red Badge of Courage* is about that." Wolden says that when he looks at old pictures of himself from Vietnam, "I see this little kid, this little nineteen-year-old kid. And yet I know how hard he was, how unfeeling he was."

He remembers one afternoon, months after Hue, when his squad gathered at the top of a small hill. American artillery was firing over their heads at an enemy position. Wolden and two other battle-seasoned marines recognized the danger of a "friendly fire" accident and hustled down the hill to take cover in a bomb crater. Minutes later, several rounds fell short, "right in the middle of our platoon."

Walking back up the hill, Wolden saw his gravely wounded squad leader, an officer he considered a "brownnoser" who often needlessly put his troops in danger. "His body was all pulled apart, but he was still breathing. My only thought was, 'Good, I don't have to deal with him anymore.'"

It wasn't the first time Wolden had lost a squad leader. In Hue an African American sergeant had "harassed me relentlessly my first four or five days," Wolden says, trying to teach the green marine how to survive. The sergeant had saved Wolden's life several times. Then, one day, a tank shell blew off the sergeant's legs. Looking down on that carnage, Wolden says, "I felt tremendously alone. What the hell was I going to do now?"

Taking off the Glasses

The sense of isolation was among the Vietnam War soldier's special agonies, Wolden says.

The well-intended policy during Vietnam was to spread the war's risks and reduce battle fatigue by requiring only one-year tours of duty in the war zone. But together with the constant losses to casualties, the frequent comings and goings meant that troops in Vietnam were commonly fighting beside relative strangers.

Wolden himself became a skilled squad leader, but "about the time I reached my peak as a soldier, I was sent back to 'the world.'"

"Vietnam was a very individual experience," Wolden says. "You went there alone and you left alone."

Upon coming home, the Vietnam War veteran remained alone, merged into a civilian population that, while preoccupied with the war as a political issue, had little firsthand knowledge of its realities.

During America's four years in World War II, by way of comparison, one-sixth of the nation's entire male population served in uniform. In more than a decade of war in Southeast Asia, barely one American male in forty set foot on Vietnamese soil, and only a fraction of those saw combat.

Wolden couldn't understand Americans' shock and outrage when, slightly more than a year after his return from Vietnam, the Kent State tragedy ended in the fatal shooting of four student war protesters by National Guard troops.

"I said to myself, 'Screw that! So four kids got shot. I've seen twenty shot a day! Big deal!' That was my thought. I couldn't put it together."

At the height of the Tet Offensive, Americans died in Vietnam at the rate of one thousand each week. Back home, Wolden thought, "We should invade Hanoi, cut off the head of the snake. Even though I knew the war was wrong, I also knew people were still dying over there."

Wolden says his anger spilled in every direction—toward war protesters, toward World War II veterans who he thought trivialized Vietnam as something less than a "real" war, toward friends and relatives, busy with "day-to-day living," who "had no clue to the depth of horror I'd been involved with. Nor did they ask. Nor did I want to tell them."

Feeling "estranged from everybody" and suffering frequent "rage fantasies," Wolden abandoned college and reenlisted in the military, where the "hard, ruthless Charlie" could prosper. He joined the air force, became a B-52 pilot and rose to the rank of major. He earned top-secret clearance and flew covert reconnaissance and combat missions in the Middle East and elsewhere.

But he remained "horrifically unhappy." Two marriages failed. During one of innumerable sleepless nights, in the mid-1980s, Wolden recognized himself in a television program about Vietnam War veterans and post-traumatic stress disorder, an emotional affliction common among survivors of overwhelming experiences.

Nearly two decades after his Vietnam War service, Wolden sought and received counseling. He left behind a distinguished military career and began a process he describes as "taking off the glasses" through which he'd seen the world ever since the day he'd noticed there was no background music in Hue.

Positive Purpose

Since 1991, Wolden has been a mental-health therapist, having earned a master's degree in the field after his air force discharge. He has worked as a child-protection social worker and today is a partner in a small rural mental-health clinic near St. Croix Falls. He specializes in work with domestic abusers and Vietnam War vets.

It is often asked why Vietnam War veterans seem to suffer more psychological problems than veterans of other wars. Wolden answers, first, that any difference is easily overstated. More than three hundred thousand psychological discharges were issued during World War II, he says.

In the late nineteenth century, Americans had noticed a strange sorrow and remoteness in many Civil War veterans. They called it "soldier's heart."

"If there's one difference between Vietnam and World War II," Wolden says, "it's that everything was justified in World War II. Atrocities American troops committed, friendly fire accidents—all of it was justified because Hitler and the Japanese had to be done in."

Charlie Wolden in 1998. The "indescribable experience" of Vietnam always will be with him, he says. Photograph by Dawn Villella for the *St. Paul Pioneer Press*.

The justice of America's cause in Vietnam was always more in doubt—even for, maybe especially for, soldiers in the field.

"We'd go into villages," Wolden remembers, "and shoot water buffalo, shoot their dogs, bayonet their pigs, do stuff to terrorize these people. And even though I was part of it, even though I knew we had to terrorize them because the Viet Cong were terrorizing them and it was a question of who was going to terrorize them the most, still I knew something was really wrong."

Confusingly, Wolden also saw in Vietnam "how good human beings can be toward one another. Us toward the Vietnamese, and the Vietnamese toward one another. I did see that, in between a lot of other stuff—but it was there."

Today, Wolden believes that America's "intent was righteous" in Vietnam, but it was a "misguided endeavor" and "wrong" to try to impose American institutions and ideas there.

Wolden says Vietnam War veterans have needed to find a "positive purpose" to their ordeal, just as other veterans did. For him, the purpose is that Vietnam taught America "nonviolence." It "doesn't mean we don't need an army," he says, but that American soldiers ought never again be sent to die and kill unnecessarily.

"Vietnam kept us out of El Salvador and Nicaragua," he says, "and got us out of Somalia quickly." Wolden says the 1991 Persian Gulf War brought Vietnam War veterans "flooding in" to counselors. It seemed to many that the nation had forgotten the lesson of Vietnam, that the "meaning was shattered again."

What Was It All About?

Vietnam War veterans do not all share a single understanding of the war's meaning, any more than other Americans do. But many veterans have shared the personal challenge Wolden describes of "having been in a situation where evil must be done. How do you come back out of that?"

The journey back, Wolden says, involves reintegrating the two halves of the self—"the ruthless, hard Charlie and the caring, compassionate Charlie . . . the hard-core combatant and the kid you were before you went. You can't give up the hard part, because it won't go away."

Wolden says that many Vietnam War vets who are doing well have found integration in "helping professions." They are cops, social workers, paramedics, "do-gooders," he says—roles where compassion and a knack for handling oneself in a crisis work together.

"What's most important is to realize I can choose who I want to be," Wolden says. "It comes down to defining values like acceptance, tolerance, capacity for love—all the stuff that was compromised in Vietnam so I could live. The big part is to get your behavior consistent with those values . . . and not to be seduced into thinking the journey has an end."

Today, in addition to his counseling work, Wolden is a contented single father to his youngest child, a teenage son. He is enthusiastically involved in politics as chairman of the Polk County Democratic Party.

"I am very pleased in my life," he says. "I'm as happy as I'm ever going to be, because I'm going to carry some of this Vietnam stuff to my grave."

So, he thinks, in some degree, will everyone who lived through those years. "I've never met anybody from back then who doesn't have some guilt," he says. "Guilt because they didn't go or guilt because they went. It was a scar on America."

Wolden says he recently saw a television interview from Vietnam with a former Viet Cong guerrilla. She was bitter about her country's establishing diplomatic relations with America and welcoming capitalist investment in Vietnam.

In a way, Wolden says, he knows how she feels.

"What was it all about?"

Dahlberg, a scarf around his neck and a champagne bottle at the ready, looks dashing here in his quarters, about 1944. Photograph courtesy of Ken Dahlberg.

WHO THE HELL IS KEN DAHLBERG?

Watergate, 1972

"You have to have a little luck in life," Ken Dahlberg likes to say. But in August 1972, Dahlberg wasn't feeling lucky.

The Twin Cities businessman was in Miami, attending the Republican National Convention. The scent of scandal was in the air. A Florida investigator tracked down Dahlberg on the convention floor and took him in for questioning.

A cashier's check for twenty-five thousand dollars, in Kenneth H. Dahlberg's name, had recently been discovered in the Miami bank account of one Bernard Barker. Barker was one of five men arrested earlier that summer attempting to burglarize the headquarters of the Democratic National Committee in Washington, D.C.'s Watergate complex.

Dahlberg was a high-ranking fund-raiser for President Richard Nixon's reelection campaign. At that early stage, the shocking truth wasn't yet clear to anyone—the truth that Dahlberg's check would break open the most devastating political scandal in American history.

The local investigator, eager to seize a moment in the national spotlight, "put me through the third degree," Dahlberg remembers. "This guy was really tough."

Driving Dahlberg back to his hotel after a grueling interrogation, the prosecutor relaxed. "I have a feeling I know you," he told Dahlberg.

"Well," Dahlberg replied, "I don't have a feeling I know you, nor do I care to know you."

The prosecutor, like Dahlberg a member of the World War II generation, persisted. "What did you do in the military?" he asked.

Dahlberg answered that he had been a fighter pilot. The investigator shook his head. That couldn't be it.

"I was a tank commander," he said. "The only pilot I knew was the dumbest shit I ever met. He got shot down during the Battle of the Bulge, crash-landed behind

Ken Dahlberg in flight gear,
1944. Photograph courtesy
of Ken Dahlberg.

German lines. My driver and I risked our lives to go rescue him. And when we get up to the plane, he's standing on the wing holding his ribs with one hand and holding a .45 in the other. He demands code words, like who pitched for the Yankees in '39. I said, 'Christ, I don't know! Get in the damn tank!' "

Dahlberg listened calmly, then asked, "How is Ralph?"

"What?"

"Ralph. Your tank driver."

The prosecutor nearly steered off the road. "You sonofabitch!" he cried. "You're the guy!"

Dahlberg later mused to reporters that, on reflection, he probably should have shot his tormentor when he had the chance. The uncanny reunion put bookends on the improbable twentieth-century adventure of Ken Dahlberg—war hero, entrepreneur, political activist, and unwitting agent of a president's destruction.

Where's the Action?

Dahlberg was born in St. Paul in 1917 and grew up on a western Wisconsin farm. "In today's world, we would be regarded as very poor," he says.

As a teenager, Dahlberg moved in with "rich relatives" in St. Paul, an uncle who was a janitor and an aunt who was a cook. After graduating from Harding High in 1935, Dahlberg found work washing pots and pans at the Lowry Hotel.

He remembers as "the biggest promotion of my life" his elevation into the lofty ranks of dishwashers. Superiors soon tapped him for more responsibility. By the time he was drafted for World War II service in 1941, Dahlberg was catering manager for a national hotel chain.

Dahlberg's "luck" included making influential acquaintances through his hotel work. Impressive references helped win him a spot as an aviation cadet. He became a flight instructor, training Chinese and American pilots in combat tactics in Arizona. He formed a friendship there with another young pilot named Barry Goldwater.

The extensive flying and gunnery practice he enjoyed as an instructor served Dahlberg well, he says, in the hazardous work that lay ahead in Europe. Goldwater's friendship would later lead him into another kind of danger.

Even as an instructor, Dahlberg was something of a daredevil. One day he crashed a plane into a power line, cutting electricity to the entire city of Yuma. Grounded and assigned to base police duty, he soon landed in the hospital after a motorcycle accident. At that point, his commanding officer told Dahlberg he was shipping him overseas and into combat "before you kill yourself."

This turn of events proved deadly for numerous German aviators. Dahlberg started flying combat missions on D-Day, protecting advancing Allied troops from German fighters while bombing and strafing Nazi airfields, trains, and other "targets of opportunity."

Dahlberg in an AT6 at the Yuma army air base, April 1943. Photograph courtesy of Ken Dahlberg.

Dahlberg says his experience as a trainer, and as a bird-hunting farm kid, made him a good shot, able to make the most of the awesome firepower of the Mustang and Thunderbolt fighters he piloted.

"When eight .50-caliber machine guns, each expending three thousand rounds a minute, converge at two hundred yards," Dahlberg remembers, "things happen."

It was almost a month before Dahlberg shot down his first Nazi plane. But having once tasted victory, he never slowed down. On two missions that summer and fall, he shot down a total of seven German fighters. Just before Christmas, during the Battle of the Bulge, he led an eight-fighter squadron into a dogfight against ninety German aircraft. Dahlberg shot down another four enemies.

By war's end, Dahlberg had destroyed fifteen Nazi planes, becoming one of a dozen triple aces in the entire American armed forces. He was awarded the Distinguished Flying Cross (twice), the Silver Star, and the Distinguished Service Cross, which stands second only to the Congressional Medal of Honor.

"I don't know how to describe it [air combat]," Dahlberg says. "There's an enormous amount of adrenaline. There's an element of fear. It's you or him, and it's not like a referee is going to step in when your three minutes are up."

Loading the machine guns of Dahlberg's fighter, 1944. Note the swastika decals on the plane, signifying Dahlberg's "kills." Photograph courtesy of Ken Dahlberg.

He remembers dogfights beginning at thirty thousand feet and leading into an earthward spiral. The key to survival was to fly a tighter spiral than the enemy and get the first shot.

Despite—or maybe because of—what one of his medal citations calls Dahlberg's "extraordinary determination to destroy the enemy," he did not always prevail. Dahlberg was shot down three times, and he says some friends argue that he should only be given credit for twelve "net" victories, having ruined three perfectly good American planes.

Twice (once with the help of his future interrogator), Dahlberg returned to duty after being shot down. But after his third crash, in February 1945, he was captured. He made several unsuccessful escape attempts, but spent the last months of the war as a POW.

Ever since his days as a fighter pilot, Dahlberg admits, life has seemed "kind of slow most of the time. I'm always wondering, 'Where's the action?' "

CREEP

Dahlberg found new fields for action in the business and political worlds.

After working for an electronics firm for several years, he founded his own company in 1948. Though not an engineer, Dahlberg had a knack for imagining what was mechanically possible, which he attributes to his farm youth.

"My father always said that 'farmers know where the handle is,' " he remembers.

The challenge of designing a better hearing aid particularly intrigued Dahlberg. Hearing aids in those days were bulky and unsightly, with a separate microphone unit typically attached to an earpiece by a cord. Dahlberg wanted to create a virtually invisible hearing aid, and someone said that if he could do that, "it would be a miracle."

An early version of the Miracle Ear, the first all-in-the-ear hearing aid, appeared in 1955.

Dahlberg's company thrived, for a time as a subsidiary of Motorola. But by the mid-1960s, events began to distract Dahlberg from his business. Aggressive antitrust regulators were moving to restrict the hearing-aid industry, complaining of high prices they blamed on manufacturers who owned exclusive retail outlets. This interference "stymied the business," Dahlberg says.

In 1964, Barry Goldwater had run unsuccessfully as the Republican candidate for president, recruiting his old air corps buddy Ken Dahlberg as a fund-raiser.

Dahlberg's business experience had stirred political frustrations over taxes and regulation. He became an enthusiastic Republican fund-raiser and organizer at both the state and national levels. In 1968, he served as a regional fund-raiser for

Dahlberg enjoys a Washington ceremony in 1968 where Vice President Hubert Humphrey made a long-delayed presentation of Dahlberg's Distinguished Service Cross, the second highest decoration the American military can bestow. Because of Dahlberg's capture at the end of the war, the medal was not presented then and had been forgotten. Though Dahlberg and Humphrey were political adversaries, they were warm personal friends. Photograph courtesy of Ken Dahlberg.

Richard Nixon's presidential campaign. Nixon narrowly defeated Vice President Hubert Humphrey of Minnesota that year.

In 1972, Dahlberg was named Midwest finance chairman for the Committee to Reelect the President, an organization that has gone down in history as CREEP.

Dahlberg admired Nixon but "never worshiped him," he says. "I got to be a junkie in my beliefs, but not toward politicians," he says. "I knew these guys, and they don't know any more than you and I know."

Fund-raising was frenetic in early 1972. In April, a new campaign finance law was to take effect, requiring increased disclosure of contributions. Donors desiring anonymity rushed to contribute before the deadline.

One of these was agribusiness tycoon Dwayne Andreas, a longtime supporter of Democrat Humphrey. Unhappy with the liberal turn the Democratic Party was taking in 1972, Andreas confidentially gave Dahlberg twenty-five thousand dollars for the Nixon war chest. Dahlberg converted the currency into a cashier's check and gave it to former commerce secretary Maurice Stans, then Nixon's national finance chairman. It was all perfectly legal.

When news broke in June about the strange break-in at the Watergate, Dahlberg had no idea his life was about to change.

Woodstein Calling

"Who the hell is Ken Dahlberg?" Richard Nixon growls in one of the infamous White House tapes that helped expose the president's wrongdoing.

Nixon had met Dahlberg, who still has his Nixon-era White House pass. But in the stress of the moment, he'd apparently forgotten him.

No one understood better than Nixon that the discovery of a CREEP fund-raiser's check in a Watergate burglar's account exposed a trail that could lead all the way to impeachment.

Nixon was a central and polarizing presence in American politics for three full decades. He became, by many assessments, a bold and capable president, at least in handling foreign affairs. Yet, his underhanded schemes to sabotage political opponents transformed him into an outlaw in the White House. Few of his transgressions were unheard-of among presidents, but their overall scale was unprecedented.

"Watergate" became the label for a tangled assortment of administration misdeeds that came to light following the famous burglary and led to the criminal convictions of more than twenty Nixon associates. The president avoided impeachment by resigning, the only president to do so, in August 1974. He was pardoned for whatever crimes he committed by his successor, Gerald Ford.

Dahlberg knew nothing of the White House skulduggery, but its unraveling began with his check. Toward the end of July 1972, he received a surprise phone call at home from "Bernstein or Woodward or Woodstein, whoever it was."

It was *Washington Post* reporter Bob Woodward, who together with partner Carl Bernstein uncovered most of the early Watergate revelations. The pivotal call to Dahlberg figures prominently in Woodward and Bernstein's book, *All the President's Men,* and in the movie based upon it.

In the film, Dahlberg's disembodied voice tells Woodward he can't talk because his neighbor has just been kidnapped. Countless filmgoers doubtless have thought this a rather creative evasion. But many Minnesotans know Dahlberg was referring to the notorious 1972 kidnapping of socialite Virginia Piper, who was ransomed for one million dollars.

Dahlberg still objects to his portrayal in the movie as fearful and flustered. "If everything in that movie is as phony as my part, the whole thing is phony," he says.

Yet Dahlberg soon became uneasy enough. "The FBI got on me; I was interrogated like mad. They had me pegged as the conduit of money from all over the world. Some was coming in from Mexico. Did I have any connections in Mexico?

Yes, we had a subsidiary there. Aha! Did I have a Swiss bank account? Yes, I owned part of a hearing-aid company there. Aha!

"That was really not nice. But I never worried. I suspect that on the larger scene, I'm suspected of being one of those bums. But I was not involved in any hanky-panky."

Prosecutors agreed, as did a Washington grand jury before which Dahlberg was called. He was never accused of wrongdoing.

Dahlberg still doubts that Nixon did anything altogether different from other presidents. Yet, he says, in another sense, "he got what he deserved. When he started out, when I first knew him, he was a very serious guy. At the end, he was getting flaky, not really coherent."

Nixon was drinking heavily by then, Dahlberg believes, a new development. "He went off his rocker, simply went off his rocker. He should have been in treatment instead of the White House that last year."

In the aftermath of Watergate, Dahlberg curtailed most political involvement, suddenly lacking any "zest or gusto" for it.

"We were going to change the world," he says.

Dahlberg admires a model of a P-51 Mustang at his Deephaven home. Photograph by Chris Polydoroff for the _St. Paul Pioneer Press_.

Higher Power

In 1983, the Reagan administration lifted restrictions on the hearing-aid industry that had prevented companies from operating their own exclusive retail outlets. Dahlberg Electronics took off, opening a thousand Miracle Ear stores and growing from thirteen million dollars in sales in 1982 to about one hundred million in 1994. That year, Dahlberg retired and sold the firm to a major manufacturer.

"All's well that ends well," Dahlberg says of his life.

The battle-scarred veteran of campaign-finance troubles watches the current campaign-finance reform debate with, well, special interest. He believes full and immediate disclosure of political contributions, not restrictions, is the answer.

"It's very corrupting," he says of money in politics. "But it's nondisclosure that's the seed of corruption."

The war hero and patriot sees broader "damage to our moral fiber" in modern Americans' eagerness to blame "corruption not on corrupt people but always on the system." He worries about what he sees as a declining work ethic, a growing sense of entitlement, and a waning spirit of individual duty.

"An individual is an incredible thing," Dahlberg says, "individuals who understand that they have power over themselves and power to do good for others."

Dahlberg remembers a game of marbles during his boyhood, when he won a piglet from another farm boy. But the piglet wasn't the loser's to gamble away. Dahlberg's father made him give it back, despite his protests that he'd won it fairly.

" 'There's a higher power than that,' my father said. 'Somebody's made a mistake. That will happen throughout life, and sometimes you'll have to pay for others' mistakes.'

"My father knew what he was talking about," Dahlberg says. "Wrong things have to be made right."

Henry Boucha during his comeback attempt with the St. Paul Fighting Saints, about 1976. Photograph courtesy of Henry Boucha.

The Long Journey of a Hockey Legend

It was early spring along the Salmon River in the mountains of central Idaho. Henry Boucha (boo-SHAY) was hiking alone across a high ridge. It was 1986. Boucha says he had felt alone for a long time, even when he had company.

"I was the sort of person who didn't talk a lot," Boucha says. "It's very difficult to sort things out by yourself. It took me a while to get my anger out. I suppose I should have had professional help."

If there is such a thing as a quintessential Minnesota fairy tale, Boucha had lived it, once upon a time. A poor Indian kid from a remote town on the Canadian border, he had grown up to become one of his state's most acclaimed hockey superstars. Conquering Minnesota high school hockey and the Olympics, he had risen to budding stardom in the National Hockey League (NHL). A boy from northern Minnesota could have imagined no more heroic destiny.

But at age twenty-four, Boucha's improbable dream-come-true had turned suddenly into a nightmare. A vicious on-ice assault with a hockey stick nearly blinded him and ended his young, charmed career.

Eleven years had passed since that disaster. Boucha says he had spent it all "lost in self-pity," wandering, drinking too much. But "I always believed in destiny," he says.

"I was on this big hill," Boucha says, "when I came around a corner and found a whole golden eagle that had died during the winter. I didn't know what to do with it."

Boucha adds with a chuckle that at the time he knew so little about his Indian heritage that he wasn't aware an Indian has a legal right to keep eagle carcasses and feathers. He worried about being prosecuted if he took the endangered bird.

But Boucha knew one thing about eagles. "The eagle is the messenger," he says, "from the Great Spirit to the people. This is gonna sound corny, but it was like a revelation to me.

"Like a call to go home."

Water and Winter

Many strands of Minnesota history come together to weave the fabric of Henry Boucha's life.

In the early 1700s, French explorers penetrated west from Lake Superior to Lake of the Woods in search of fish, fur, and timber. They found the longtime resident Dakota Indians living in uneasy peace beside the Ojibwe, who had recently migrated to the area, driven west by white settlement. The arrival of European traders kindled competition between the tribes, and soon warfare.

Many northern Minnesota place-names are thought to have originated in events of the Dakota-Ojibwe wars—Battle River, Thief River, Red Lake. There was also a trail leading west from Lake of the Woods that became a common route for war parties heading into battle. The Ojibwe called it Kah-bay-kah-nong, which the French translated as Chemin de Guerre.

Later, in English, it became "war road."

Henry Boucha was born in the small, lakeside town of Warroad, Minnesota, in 1951. His mother was Ojibwe; his father, a French-Canadian fisherman, trapper, and logger. Boucha was the eighth of nine children. Several cousins also grew up in the Bouchas' two-bedroom house. The family was "fairly poor," Boucha says, yet it was "good living." Fish and game were abundant, and "we basically grew up on walleye," Boucha says.

As a boy, Boucha loved boating on the vast, island-filled lake and spending whole summers at remote fishing camps, even though he had a slight tendency toward seasickness. "I like water even better when it's frozen," Boucha says.

It is often frozen around Warroad. Almost as soon as he could walk, Boucha took up the passion that has naturally, almost inevitably, become an obsession among northern Minnesotans—inhabitants of a landscape whose controlling features are water and winter.

"Hockey was all we had to do," Boucha remembers. "We went to school, came home, put our skates on, and made our own fun." Warroad kids played hockey on the lake and on the river. When ice conditions weren't right, they'd play in their boots on the road. A snuff can wrapped in tape served as a puck, slapped around with makeshift sticks held together with nails and tape.

"Even when I was four or five years old," Boucha remembers, "the older kids would always be short one player. They'd need a goalie. So they'd come in and ask my mom and she'd dress me up and I'd take a little stick out there and stand in the goal. I'd come in with welts all over my body and forehead. But they said I didn't cry too often."

While sharing the dream of hockey greatness that haunted every Warroad boy, Boucha mostly rejected his Indian heritage, as did many Indian kids who lived off reservations in those days. "It was embarrassing watching those old John Wayne movies," Boucha says. "There wasn't anything to be proud about because of the mass put-down of Indians by society. Hell no, I didn't want to be an Indian."

Even today, Boucha worries about severe social problems and ineffective governments on reservations. He still sees, as he did in his own youth, "a big difference between reservation kids and those in the Warroad area." Assimilation into the larger American society, he says, "is obviously better to a degree. But it doesn't mean Indians have to throw away their heritage and traditions."

Boucha regrets that he allowed it to mean just that when he was growing up. His mother, who wanted her children to assimilate, also wanted to teach them the Ojibwe language. "But I didn't want to learn it," Boucha says.

Athletic skills he mastered. Coaches and fans soon started comparing Boucha to the legendary Indian athlete Jim Thorpe. As a twelve-year-old, Boucha led a Warroad bantam hockey team to the state championship. At Warroad High School, he became a star sprinter on the track team, a dangerous slugger on the baseball team, and a precise placekicker on the football team who was offered a scholarship by Notre Dame.

But it was his swift, graceful skating on the hockey rink, his instinct for being where the puck was, his stinging backhand, that got people talking about Boucha's potential for real athletic greatness, for the big leagues. He was named to Minnesota's all-state hockey team as a sophomore, junior, and senior. In his senior year, 1969, Boucha led Warroad to the state hockey tournament.

His legend, along with his bad luck, was about to begin.

Electricity

All the ingredients for high athletic melodrama were present in the state high school hockey tournament in 1969.

Those were the days of a one-class tournament. Tiny Warroad High School, with fewer than two hundred students, had arrived to challenge city and suburban schools ten times its size. There was even the outside chance of a showdown between the backwoods Cinderella favorites and Edina. The large, affluent suburban school was in those days something of an athletic dynasty, a perennial powerhouse in various sports that many fans and sportswriters loved to root against.

It was also the first year the tournament was played at the new, and since demolished, Metropolitan Sports Center in Bloomington. Record attendance followed, as did heightened interest from the public and the press.

And then there were the stories preceding Henry Boucha, the Indian youngster from Warroad who skated, said one inspired Twin Cities sportswriter, with "the silvery stride" of "an antelope." The coach of the Minnesota North Stars added that Boucha already had a stronger backhand than anyone on Minnesota's young NHL team.

Both Boucha and the tournament lived up to expectations.

In Warroad's opening game, Boucha scored the winning goal in the final period to upset powerful Minneapolis Southwest. Next, Warroad met its larger rival from the north, Roseau. Boucha played the entire game, never taking a rest. Again, in the final period, Boucha sped the length of the rink, slipped past defenders and scored the winning goal as Warroad earned the right to advance to the finals against Edina, which had made short work of its first two opponents.

Few events in Minnesota sports history have exceeded the anticipation and emotional intensity of that Warroad-Edina final. "You could feel the electricity in that building," Boucha remembers. "It was one of the biggest highlights of my life." No game he ever played in the Olympics or the NHL compared with the thrill of that March evening, he says.

Against the odds, Boucha and Warroad gave Edina everything it could handle. Edina led 2–1 in the second period when Boucha and an Edina defenseman raced after the puck into a corner behind the Edina net. In the collision that followed, Boucha's head was slammed against the glass above the boards. He crumpled to the ice, with a concussion and a broken eardrum. He was immediately taken to a hospital, where he stayed for three days. His $1,500 bill was paid by contributions from the citizens of Warroad.

Boucha has never complained about that incident, which he considers a hard but fair hit. The crowd felt differently. For the rest of the game and on into the tournament award ceremony, the Edina team was roundly booed.

Meanwhile, Boucha's teammates took inspiration from their star's injury and battled heroically, tying the game and sending it into overtime. Edina finally prevailed 5–4, but it was Boucha and Warroad who had won the hearts of Minnesotans.

In the next few years, Boucha's dreams came true in rapid succession. He traveled the world, playing for the U.S. National Team in 1970 and 1971. He was the

The Warroad High School
hockey team, sentimental
favorites at the 1969 state
tournament. Boucha is in
the back row, sixth from
left. *St. Paul Pioneer Press*
file photo.

top scorer on the 1972 Olympic team, which won a surprising silver medal in
Sapporo, Japan. That year he was drafted by the NHL's Detroit Red Wings. He
became Detroit's rookie of the year and was quickly developing into an NHL star
when he was traded to the Minnesota North Stars for the 1974–75 season.

"I was just elated to come back to my home state," Boucha says. "Everything
was going as planned. I was working my way up to some really good bargaining
power."

Boucha wore his hair fashionably long at the time. He took to wearing a large
sweatband around his head to keep perspiration out of his eyes. (Few hockey players wore helmets in those years.) Many interpreted Boucha's headband as a kind
of Indian costume, and some Indian advocates criticized Boucha for exploiting his
heritage. He shrugged off the complaints and marketed paper headbands as fan
novelties.

Boucha was earning $105,000 a year when he came to the North Stars—a
handsome sum by NHL standards of the time. He says with a smile that he grieves
about what happened that winter "even more now that the average NHL salary is
$1.5 million."

Beyond Reason

"I'm glad they tore it down," Boucha says of Met Center. "I got hurt there in '69
and again in '75. If I'd been standing there when they blew it up, it probably would
have fallen over on me."

On January 4, 1975, the North Stars played a game at Met Center against the
Boston Bruins, a team notorious for the brawling that often despoils NHL hockey.
A rough young Boston player named Dave Forbes "was shadowing me the whole
game," Boucha remembers, "yapping, throwing elbows." Inevitably, Boucha and

Forbes ended up dropping their gloves and slugging it out. Both were sent to the penalty box.

Some minutes later, both returned to the ice. "I looked over at him," Boucha says, "and it didn't look like he was going to do anything. So I looked back at the coach."

Just then, Forbes rushed over and slammed the butt end of his stick into Boucha's face. People all over the arena heard the bones of Boucha's eye socket snap as he fell in a heap on the ice, with a cut requiring thirty stitches and irreversible damage to the muscles controlling his right eye.

Boucha underwent three surgeries and tried to return to the game. But his hockey career was over; he suffers impaired vision to this day.

So beyond reason was Forbes's attack on Boucha that the Hennepin County Attorney filed aggravated assault charges against the Boston player. His trial ended in a hung jury. After five years of bitter litigation against the Bruins, Forbes, and the NHL, Boucha won a settlement that still provides him with annual compensation.

Meanwhile, the twenty-four-year-old hockey legend suddenly faced the toughest and least expected comeback challenge of his life—the challenge of finding a new dream and a new identity.

Success

"You spend a lifetime building a reputation," Boucha says, "and you can blow it all in a couple of hours. Then you spend the rest of your life trying to make up for your ignorance and pride."

For more than a decade after his career-ending injury, Boucha wandered impulsively, from the West Coast back to Detroit, back to Warroad, and out to Idaho. He invested in a series of ill-considered business ventures and, by his own account, spent too much time drinking excessively, "crying in my beer," and "getting ornery." His behavior, he says, "didn't sit well with the people of Warroad, and it didn't sit well with me."

Right out of high school, Boucha had married a hometown sweetheart, but his nomadic life as a hockey player had quickly undone the marriage. During his NHL days, he wed for a second time, marrying a "city gal" and model, he says, with whom he had little in common once he was no longer part of the professional sports world. That marriage ended in 1979. Soon after that, he met his current wife, Elaine, whom he gives great credit for "standing by me" during "pretty trying times emotionally."

Boucha and Elaine with former North Stars coach Glen Sonmor (left) and NHL great Gordie Howe, 1994. Photograph courtesy of Henry Boucha.

Boucha says the peacefulness and closeness to nature of his years in Idaho with Elaine, who shares his love of the outdoors, had begun to bring his blurred vision of life back into focus by the time he found the dead eagle. That "revelation" helped him decide to return once again to Warroad, to reconnect with family and his heritage, and to seek "a new way of looking at success" by trying to help young people who were like he was as a boy.

Boucha moved back to Warroad in the late 1980s. He went into the real estate business and became a leader in efforts to help Indian children. In 1993, Boucha founded an Indian education program in the Warroad public schools and ran the organization for four years, intervening in Indian students' problems at school and at home. He calls it both the most rewarding and the most stressful work of his life.

Boucha's own four children have returned to live with him in Warroad at various times. He had far too little contact with them during his years on the road, he says. His youngest, J.P., ten years old, is a budding hockey star.

In 1998, Boucha founded a new nonprofit agency, called Kah-bay-kah-nong, to provide umbrella fund-raising and management for his various interests. These include an annual Warroad powwow; a diversity hockey program and an Indian youth hockey program, both blessed with Boucha as a coach and inspirational leader; and a research organization studying the history of Indian people in the Warroad area.

Delighted with the new pride Indians have come to feel in recent decades, and the new respect they have come to receive from the larger society, Boucha says he is finally at peace.

"I've come to terms with my injury. There are many ways to look at success. I've got my role as a grandpa and a dad, keeping the family close knit. I always believed I was here for a purpose, and helping people is the greatest satisfaction in life. I'd like to continually learn more about my heritage. My hockey career is long over with."

But if Boucha's real everyday heroism emerged through his recovery from the tragic end of his playing days, his grace and guts on the hockey rink have never been forgotten by those who witnessed them.

In 1995, Henry Boucha was inducted into the U.S. Hockey Hall of Fame.

Grandfather Pham (lower right) in ceremonial dress at a family wedding in 1969. Pham Duc Loi is in the top row, second from right. Photograph courtesy of Luu Pham.

Saigon to Minneapolis

Luu Pham's only memories of his homeland are fragmentary, shadowy images.

The young Minneapolis playwright and actor remembers a swing in the small courtyard of his family's Saigon home. He remembers a path that led to a park and a soccer field. He remembers riding between his father's legs on a small motorcycle.

Pham also remembers the day he departed on an exciting trip with his brothers and sisters, mother and grandfather. They boarded a "big, dark airplane" that had no seats, just a vast cavity, as if the family had been swallowed by a whale.

The four-year-old boy had no knowledge of the panic that gripped Saigon that April day in 1975, when his family fled the city aboard an American cargo plane. Communist North Vietnamese troops were closing in on the capital of South Vietnam. Its conquest days later would bring an end to more than a century of struggle for control of Indochina.

Generations of Luu Pham's family fought in that struggle, always on the defeated side.

"I empathize with the generation of Americans who went through the Vietnam War," Pham says. "They're haunted by the same thing I am." Yet most Americans, he suspects, "don't even know the history I'm haunted by."

At every stage of America's development, the nation has been home to haunted newcomers—recent refugee immigrants who, while happy to escape wars, oppressions, and hardships, have also suffered the agonies of being violently cut off from their home, their culture, their heritage. As the twenty-first century begins, more than one million Southeast Asian refugees (many thousands of them in Minnesota) are among those carrying on this distinctive and poignant American tradition.

Luu Pham and his sister Mai Linh in the courtyard of their Saigon home, 1974. Photograph courtesy of Luu Pham.

"It's a strange thing," says Pham, who has written three plays about his family's past. "I don't know why I carry this history with me." He's linked to the past, he says, by close relationships with his grandfather and mother. But perhaps most important is "the relationship I have with my father, which developed out of his absence."

Pham has no memory of saying goodbye to his father, or of being aware that his father—a scholar, poet, and soldier—was not accompanying the family on its hurried flight from besieged Saigon.

They would never see him again.

Mad in Your Stomach

Pham Dinh Lieu, Luu Pham's grandfather, has traced their family's lineage back to fifteenth-century Vietnam, when an ancestor named Mac ruled briefly as emperor, but was soon deposed. Afterward, the clan changed its name to escape political reprisals.

Persecution was still a hazard four centuries later, when Grandfather Pham was born in 1904 in a village not far from Hanoi in northern Vietnam. France had imposed colonial rule on Vietnam in the 1860s. From the beginning, the Pham clan of what Luu Pham calls "scholar gentry" was active in a nationalist resistance movement.

Speaking through an interpreter at his North Minneapolis home, Grandfather Pham says his own grandfather—Luu Pham's great-great-grandfather—was a scholar and government official who refused to work for the French when they took power. Instead, he took part in an unsuccessful uprising against the invaders.

When he was growing up, Grandfather Pham says, "the French looked at the Vietnamese as slaves. They didn't treat you with any dignity or respect."

Education was severely restricted, a painful deprivation in scholarly, literate Vietnamese culture. Taxes were punitive. The traditional village-based social order was overthrown, and all political power was denied to the Vietnamese. The economy stagnated, and poverty persisted as France extracted raw materials from its colony.

At all this, says Grandfather Pham, "you could only get mad in your stomach. You couldn't do anything. All we had was knives. We had no guns."

Even so, the spirit of rebellion grew, fueled by a "look to the east" movement that took heart from Japan's victory in a 1905 war against Russia. The movement hoped to restore the traditional Asian social order throughout the colonized continent.

Grandfather Pham's father was imprisoned for resistance activities. His oldest brother fled to the hills to join revolutionary fighters. One day, his mother was arrested by the French and led off in shackles to be interrogated.

Luu Pham, at right, and his grandfather, Pham Dinh Lieu, in 1998. Photograph by Scott Takushi for the *St. Paul Pioneer Press.*

"After that," says Grandfather Pham, "when anybody talked about making revolution and fighting the French, I liked it. I was ready. By and by, I became a revolutionary."

In the late 1920s, Grandfather Pham was among several dozen young idealists who founded the VNQDD, the Vietnamese Nation People's Party. The group had little in the way of political ideology, beyond a desire to oust the French and restore traditional Vietnamese culture. Vaguely socialistic and democratic, the nationalists "had no idea about communism," says Grandfather Pham. "We looked for fighting spirit, the spirit to get something done. Communism? We didn't know anything about that."

Other Vietnamese rebels did, often those who had been educated in France and had encountered Marxist philosophy there. Under one of those Paris-educated radicals, Ho Chi Minh, Vietnamese communists were also organizing in the 1920s. But it was the VNQDD that acted first.

Grandfather Pham's role was to buy guns, grenades, and other weapons from sympathetic Vietnamese soldiers in the French colonial army. In 1929, VNQDD operatives assassinated a prominent French industrialist. Soon after, the group led a military uprising that failed when the French were tipped off about the plan.

"If we do not succeed, at least we will become men," said Nguyen Thai Hoc, leader of the VNQDD, before the doomed uprising. His declaration became famous among the Vietnamese.

"That kind of bravery was very common," Grandfather Pham says. "We were all willing to do things like that. And Nguyen Thai Hoc had a remarkable, awe-inspiring spirit."

The VNQDD leader died on the guillotine after the rebellion's failure, as did many others. Thousands more, including Grandfather Pham, were imprisoned in a severe wave of repression.

He spent two years in a cell one meter wide and two meters long, often sharing it with other prisoners. Beatings were common, but "they never really went to extremes with me," he says.

The VNQDD was "nothing like before" after its failed rebellion, says Grandfather Pham. Neither was his life. Dispossessed and blacklisted, he struggled to support his family through menial labor and became disillusioned with politics. The nationalist movement splintered into hostile factions, each with its own religious or political philosophy, some of them fascist.

"I never swore allegiance to any of these groups," Grandfather Pham says. "I didn't believe in that."

Least of all did he and other traditional nationalists believe in the doctrines of the communists. "Their philosophy is materialism," Grandfather Pham says. "But there's more to life. We emphasized the moral quality, the spirit. They focused on property relationships, and we rejected that."

When the French tried to reinstate colonial rule after the famines and chaos of Japanese occupation during World War II, the well-organized communists under Ho Chi Minh seized leadership of the Vietnamese resistance movement. For a time, they disavowed Marxist ideology while killing and jailing nationalists who opposed them.

Grandfather Pham was arrested by the communists, as he had been earlier by the French, but was soon released. He came to believe that Ho Chi Minh "was going to win because he was so devilishly manipulative and effective."

But Grandfather Pham "never followed the communists" or changed his view that Ho was "a very deceitful, devious person" and that "communist theory was all a lie." The communists "killed lots of people," he says.

By the time the French gave up their fight to control Indochina in 1954, Vietnam was bitterly divided between communist loyalists and a disorganized opposition of Catholic converts and various old-line nationalists. An agreement was made to partition the country into a communist North Vietnam and an independent South Vietnam.

Grandfather Pham took his family to the South.

Tender Access

As a boy growing up in America in the late 1970s, Luu Pham entertained "a child's fantasies of going back and doing something heroic to rescue my father from Vietnam."

He had been told his father was dead, but the reality only "really landed" when his father's ashes were sent to America in 1980 and the Buddhist family performed a consecration ritual. That same year, the family moved from the West Coast to the Twin Cities.

Pham Duc Loi, Luu Pham's father and Grandfather Pham's son, enlisted in the South Vietnamese Army in the mid-1950s, shortly after his family had fled the communist north. He rose rapidly in rank to lieutenant colonel.

As American involvement in the renewed war between South Vietnam and North Vietnam grew throughout the 1960s, Pham Duc Loi traveled several times to the United States for special training. He participated in peace negotiations in Paris that led to a cease-fire agreement in 1972.

Through all those years of war, Pham Duc Loi also pursued what Luu Pham calls his "artistic and literary ambitions" as a well-respected poet and scholar. All his father's works, Pham says, had a political and cultural mission, to urge unity among Southeast Asians and to support the preservation of a distinctive Vietnamese culture focused on family and community.

Pham Duc Loi decried "the devil of the American dollar" and the advance in South Vietnam of Western-style capitalism "as something just as destructive as communism to Vietnamese society," according to Luu Pham.

"I was searching for a human being I could connect with," Luu Pham says of his boyish thoughts about his father. It was to the artist and philosopher in the man that the son was drawn.

In 1989, when Pham was in college, his mother finally shared with him Pham Duc Loi's final letter to his seven children. It had been written in April 1975.

North Vietnam had that year renewed its attack on the South. America, by then paralyzed by dissension over its role in the war, did not intervene. In the final days before Saigon's fall, American officials offered Pham Duc Loi a chance to send his family to the United States. In a hasty decision, the family was rushed to the airport and boarded the cargo plane Luu Pham vaguely recalls.

The letter Pham's father wrote soon thereafter took the form of a fable. "A hermit," Luu Pham says, "had many books and a vast store of knowledge. But something was missing, something in his heart was stirring, trying to come out."

What emerged were "seven celestial bodies, seven stars. They flew into the heavens and illuminated parts of the Earth that had been dark for eons."

The hermit was overjoyed, until he noticed that the stars "had reversed their course, and were coming back to him, back to their place of origin. He realized

Pham Duc Loi in uniform, about 1956. The South Vietnamese army officer represented the fourth generation of the Pham family to fight in the struggle for Vietnam that began with French colonization in the 1860s. Photograph courtesy of Luu Pham.

there was something about him that was pulling them back. So he took poisoned honey and died and turned to dust, and the stars resumed their course.

"But each year, on their great cycle, the stars return to that place and pause momentarily, over the spot where he had stood, and then they continue."

Sometime soon after writing that letter, faced with imprisonment or execution, Pham Duc Loi took his own life.

"That gave me access to the moment," Luu Pham says. "Very tender access to what he might have been thinking and feeling." It sealed Pham's decision to "take on writing as a legacy that I wanted to follow."

Exile

Three autobiographical Luu Pham plays have been professionally staged in the Twin Cities. In one play, a grandfather tells a grandson about his youthful passion for a failed anticolonial insurrection. In another, a father's ashes are consecrated amid flashbacks to the day he spirited his family out of danger on a cargo plane. In a third, an artist strives to understand the meaning of her parents' wartime experiences in Vietnam and her father's suicide.

As an actor, Pham has appeared in his own plays and others at a number of Twin Cities theaters. He is among the founders of Pangea World Theater, an international theater company devoted, Pham says, to producing "an alignment of vision" across diverse national traditions.

"Having seen what nationalism creates," Pham says, "having seen what ideology creates, I'm trying to create a different community."

Pham observes that in many families, a young person might be discouraged from pursuing a chancy artistic career. But his grandfather, Pham says, has always urged him "to live the life of the spirit, to follow that calling."

Meanwhile, the political and social theme of his work "comes from my father," Pham says. "That was the nature of his art. Art had to make an impact. It was about transforming the nation and culture he was a part of."

The heir to four generations of unsuccessful revolution and resistance still searches for his own identity, his own relationship to the tragedy of his homeland and forebears. Pham says he has stopped referring to himself as an "Asian American" or "Vietnamese American." He says he feels "more whole than that."

"All these things are part of the continuum I live in," Pham says. "There's no attempt on my part to connect things in a conscious way. It's just who I am. I write in English about Vietnamese history. That's who I am."

The distinctive Vietnamese worldview his father and grandfather defended, Pham says, is rooted in "the abiding sense of the self as part of a continuum. What-

Luu Pham and his mother, Minh Hien Thi Nguyen, after resettling in America, about 1979. A year later, the family moved to Minnesota. Photograph courtesy of Luu Pham.

ever I am right now is just a drop in a much vaster ocean. Even when the previous generations have passed away, there's still a relationship."

Pham admires, even envies, his grandfather, who is "still so vibrant and present to life. There's something in the historical sense of his life that's whole, despite the ruptures. He understands that continuum and his place in it."

Pham thinks the strength and stoicism he sees in his grandfather and mother "is often true of displaced people. But it's not so true of the next generation, which is always searching for a reason." He says that, in a way, he has a more tragic sense of Vietnamese history than his grandfather does.

"Maybe it's a personal tragedy because I don't have that access. My grandfather is an exile, but he is not defeated by his exile. I don't know if I'm an exile, but I definitely feel distant from something I should be closer to."

Grandfather Pham says he hopes to live a few more years to see some of the new century.

"We thank you Americans," he says. "We're very grateful to be over here. If I hadn't come to America, in the hands of the communists I would have died. The damage has been to the spirit and the pride. But all my grandchildren respect me, and here they can all study and have a career."

The old revolutionary has visited the National Vietnam Veterans Memorial in Washington, D.C. He grieves for America's losses in the Vietnam struggle, along with all the other losses.

Noting that America outlasted communism in the Soviet Union, Grandfather Pham adds, "I'm very sorry America didn't have that kind of power in Asia."

Tractors lay siege to the state capitol. Political activism helped win legislation to slow foreclosures, but it's not clear how many farms were saved. *St. Paul Pioneer Press* file photo.

The Farm Crisis That Never Ended

The ringing of the telephone—harsh and urgent, as it always seems late at night—jarred Delores Swoboda awake at 2 A.M.

It was 1986, or maybe 1987. Swoboda can't be sure. In those years, it had gotten to be a habit, receiving phone calls at all hours.

In a moment, Swoboda was calm—comfortable in the darkness of the old farmhouse where she had lived for decades. She also knew what the burden of the phone call was likely to be.

It was likely to be some farmer, or some farmer's wife, panic-stricken over the impending foreclosure of the family farm and needing help, needing to talk. Swoboda was a board member and leader of the farm activist group Groundswell. She had become an unofficial counselor and comforter to hundreds of troubled Minnesota farmers.

By phone or across her big kitchen table, Swoboda was the first person many western Minnesota farmers had told about their financial troubles. Such admissions came hard.

Swoboda remembers how, after idly chatting for a time, she'd often have to casually ask a farmer how he was faring. He'd usually say things were fine.

"And I'd say: 'Boy, you're one of the lucky ones,'" Swoboda remembers. "'Cripes, the last 582 people who called here were having a heck of a time.'"

"Sometimes," Swoboda says, "that would break them down." They'd start talking about their problem.

Though she remembers one heartbreaking phone call especially well, Swoboda says urgent conversations were nothing exceptional in those years of the "farm crisis" of the middle 1980s. It was the worst financial panic American farmers had suffered since the Great Depression of the 1930s.

Delores Swoboda, farm wife and political activist, aboard an antique tractor. Farmers, she says, love their life and are determined to solve the seemingly endless problems of the family farm economy. Photograph courtesy of Delores Swoboda.

Debt Fever

Swoboda was born at the depression's end, in June 1939, on a farm ten miles south of Redwood Falls, Minnesota. It stood about fifteen miles from the farm on which she lives today.

In her youth, Swoboda moved often, from one rented farm to another. Her father was a hardscrabble dairy man who never could quite make a success of his farming. After trying six different farms on the flat, open prairie of Redwood County, the family moved north about a hundred miles to the more rolling country of Todd County.

To farm people, with roots as deep as oak trees, it was like moving to another continent. "My Dad was always lost up north," Swoboda says. With all those "crooked roads and lots of trees," her father "was never sure which end of the world the sun came up on. It just wasn't home. So when he lost his farm, we moved back to Redwood Falls."

In 1959, Delores married Gene Swoboda, whose roots ran deeper still. Gene was already farming land near Olivia that had been in his family for four generations.

"I swore to God I'd never marry a farmer," Delores recalls. "But he was kind of a nice guy. And I probably had some of that farming blood in me.

"We decided that if Gene's grandfather could raise his family and survive on this land, like his father before him, then by God we're going to do that same thing."

Farms and farmers have been disappearing for generations, and their disappearance has been lamented for generations. More productive modern machinery and methods have reduced the need for farmworkers and have caused crop prices to fall, making small farms less profitable. Especially since World War II, farm size has grown as the population living on the land has shrunk.

The 1980s farm crisis was a particularly acute and well-publicized bout with an economic virus that has been killing small farms throughout much of the twentieth century.

What happened was that a speculative fever broke, leaving behind an epidemic of insolvency. Swoboda remembers how, in the inflationary 1970s, "we would get letters from the bank or some realtor telling us about some piece of land for sale. They would be happy to finance us for that project. Or they'd say, 'Look here, you're worth three million dollars with your machinery and land. There's no reason why you can't afford a new house or machine shed or a $70,000 tractor.'"

Land values were soaring. The average price of a Minnesota acre nearly tripled between 1974 and 1981. A bigger-is-better rush was on to buy more land and the equipment to farm it, encouraged by some agricultural economists as the way to

A failing Stearns County farm is auctioned off by a deputy sheriff in September 1985. On the courthouse steps, protesters kneel and pray, including, at right, Paul Wellstone, later elected U.S. senator. The farm crisis of the 1980s attracted concern from diverse political interests, as the agrarian movement always has. Photograph from AP/Wide World Photos; reprinted with permission.

save family farming. Total U.S. farm real-estate debt doubled between 1975 and 1982.

Then the bubble burst. As land prices plummeted as fast as they'd risen (by 1987, they were back at the mid-1970s level), "lenders realized that farmers were very deep in debt," Swoboda says. "They'd borrowed way too much against the land, now that it had been devalued."

Making matters worse, interest rates spiraled higher as federal officials battled inflation. Soon, widespread farm foreclosures began.

"The Rochester newspaper," Swoboda remembers, "had seventy-five foreclosure notices in one edition."

Out of that chaos, Groundswell grew.

Sugar and Honey

Groundswell emerged from a demonstration at the state capitol in St. Paul on January 21, 1985. Called by a coalition of farm advocacy groups to demand relief from farm foreclosures, it was one of the largest capitol demonstrations ever. Afterward, the Groundswell organization was established to continue the effort.

Swoboda was at the big demonstration. She had long been writing newsletters and handling media relations for advocacy groups seeking better utility service and pollution control in rural areas. Soon she was doing similar work for Groundswell and was on the new organization's board.

Over the years, Swoboda would attend and help organize at least fifty demonstrations at farm-foreclosure auctions—Groundswell's most visible and controversial activities. Four times Swoboda was among demonstrators arrested.

Yet, Swoboda isn't much of a radical. She remembers with frustration how, in the first years of the movement, some Groundswell members would level harsh, partisan criticism at legislators, especially Republicans, and only succeed in undermining support for their proposals.

"There are better ways to tell people they're doing a rotten job," Swoboda says, "ways that are all mixed up with sugar and honey."

Groundswell also was troubled in its early days by controversy surrounding Bobbi Polzine, the group's most outspoken early leader. Eventually, Polzine was ousted from the organization because of radical political leanings that were symbolized for many by several mysterious trips she took to Nicaragua, then governed by a communist regime.

"Here's a lady who couldn't pay her telephone bill," Swoboda remembers. "Who never had a dime to pay for a meal or anything. How'd she get to Nicaragua? She'd never tell."

As Groundswell mastered the "sugar and honey" approach to its political activism, it scored some legislative successes. Swoboda never supported the more extreme call for a "moratorium" on farm foreclosures that many in Groundswell backed. But she points proudly to legislation that requires mediation between farm lenders and farmers before foreclosure, and other measures that help farmers to work out debt problems when possible. Minnesota's laws became models for similar legislation in other states and in Congress, Swoboda says.

Swoboda can't be sure whether many farms were saved by the new laws. But mediation, she thinks, helped slow the pace of foreclosures and ease the panic atmosphere. She and Gene went into mediation on their own place in 1987, and Swoboda says it was a painful ordeal. But they had not taken on major debt, and they were able to sell a modest acreage to repair their farm's balance sheet.

The crowd begins to gather for an anniversary farm rally on the state capitol steps, January 21, 1986. From a similar rally a year earlier, the Groundswell organization emerged to seek legislative relief for troubled farmers. *St. Paul Pioneer Press* file photo.

Quietness

From its organized beginnings more than a century ago, the "farm movement" or "agrarian" movement has sprawled across the American political landscape, attracting at times everyone from socialists to white separatists.

So it was in the 1980s. Jesse Jackson, Paul Wellstone, and other liberal political figures supported Groundswell's efforts and attended rallies and protests. Country and rock musicians led by Willie Nelson put on Farm Aid in 1985, a concert to support America's threatened farmers.

But Swoboda also remembers one sheriff who fearfully asked, before a foreclosure demonstration, just how many people from the right-wing Posse Comitatus Swoboda was expecting to attend. She told him there better not be many or she was going home.

For her part, Swoboda shares the farm movement's bedrock belief that growers need to receive prices for their crops that keep family farms viable. But Swoboda's personal focus has largely been on easing the human anguish of the farm troubles. "Like if we could, in six months, make ten people feel better about themselves," she says.

For Swoboda, the key purpose of the foreclosure demonstrations was not to interfere with legal processes or make sheriffs' lives miserable, although there were ugly confrontations on some occasions. Her purpose was to communicate with "farmers who weren't there and maybe thought we were a bunch of radical fools."

"We didn't have any money to write a letter to every farmer or to buy TV time. But we were pretty sure the local press would come over to a demonstration and take a picture and maybe talk to one of us."

In fact, Groundswell protests attracted statewide, national, and even international attention. The message Swoboda hoped would reach farmers was this: "If you're in trouble, there's no need for you to have a nervous breakdown or to shoot somebody or knock off a bank. What you need to do if you're in financial trouble is don't blame yourself and talk to somebody."

Swoboda says a "quietness" fueled by embarrassment keeps many financially strapped farmers isolated. She thinks the silence is inspired by a modern value system where "being poor is the only sign of human frailty."

"We're very understanding nowadays if a marriage breaks down," Swoboda says. "And if you have an alcohol problem, that's a disease. But if your house is rundown, if you're driving a car that's full of rust, you are considered a failure and you better hang your head in shame."

Swoboda says people "have to learn what their position is in life." They need to resist the temptation to live "a Cadillac lifestyle on a Chevy income" by amassing debt to collect possessions they don't really own.

"Being a big shot" that way, she says, "will get you driving a truck instead of farming."

Family Ties

It was a familiar voice on the line that late night when Delores Swoboda was awakened by the telephone. It was a struggling farmer she had been talking to for more than a year. He had often felt hopeless, even suicidal, ashamed that all the neighboring farmers seemed to be thriving.

That night, he could scarcely talk. He had just returned from the nearby farm of his best friend. The friend's wife had come home from her job and found, to her complete surprise, a foreclosure notice on the kitchen table. Then, she found her husband's body in the basement, where he had shot himself.

"I just came home from wiping him off the basement walls," the farmer told Swoboda.

The dead man had told no one of his mounting financial crisis. Not his wife, not his friend.

"I don't think I'll ever forget that," Swoboda says. "To think that man held that all inside and never said anything to anybody."

For Swoboda, this is only one more story showing that "there's a difference between a farmer losing the family farm and somebody who started up a Dairy Queen franchise and couldn't make it go." The difference has to do with "those family ties. Your great-grandfather farmed there and all that."

	1900	Today
Farm population as percent of U.S. total	41.9%	1.9%
Number of farms (U.S.)	5.7 million	1.9 million
Average size of Minnesota farm	170 acres	342 acres

Sources: U.S. Bureau of the Census, *Statistical Abstract of the United States, Historical Statistics of the United States*. The "Today" column shows the most recent figures available at time of writing.

Swoboda knows the future of the family farm remains uncertain. Groundswell, she says, has had some successes "teaching people in rural areas and small towns about the need to care about each other, to work together. We're just bound and determined that we're going to solve some of these issues one way or another."

In 1998, precipitous declines in commodity prices again endangered thousands of Minnesota farms. Swoboda reported that "it's a darned crisis again—and my phone is ringing off the wall. I think I'm gonna run away."

Farm people simply love their life, Swoboda says. "It's a big hullabaloo when they end up with six sets of twin lambs or seventeen baby pigs. They like the smell of ground turning over behind the plow. The family is doing everything together. You can look out the door and there's your husband out there in the field. He can look up to the house and there you are out working in the garden."

Today, the Swobodas' son, Don, works the ancestral farm alongside his parents. Don's youngest son "is convinced he wants to be a farmer," Swoboda says.

If the boy's farming ambition lasts, Swoboda's grandson would represent a sixth generation of the same family working the same plot of Minnesota earth.

"And wouldn't that just be something," Swoboda says.

D. J. TICE has been a writer, editor, and publisher for newspapers and magazines since 1979. He has worked with *Corporate Report, TWA Ambassador, Twin Cities Magazine,* and the *Twin Cities Reader,* and since 1991 he has been a writer and member of the editorial board at the *St. Paul Pioneer Press*. He is the coauthor (with Bonnie Blodgett) of *At Home with the Presidents.*